Living in the DEEP BRAIN

Connecting with Your Intuition

Living in the
DEEP BRAIN

Connecting with
Your Intuition

RORY MILLER

http://chirontraining.com
http://wyrdgoat.com

Cover design, interior design and graphics by Kamila Miller
http://kzmiller.com
Cover and Interior Image by Surya Prakosa

ISBN: 978-1-952110-00-9
First print edition

Disclaimer:
Information in this book is distributed "As Is," without warranty. Nothing in this document constitutes a legal opinion nor should any of its contents be treated as such. Neither the authors nor the publisher shall have any liability with respect to information contained herein. Further, neither the author, course designers, nor the publisher have any control over or assume any responsibility for websites or external resources referenced in this book.

Table of Contents

Introduction to the Introduction

Once upon a time, I woke up with an idea about writing an article for *Conflict Manager* magazine about methods to train your intuition. Gavin DeBecker's seminal *The Gift of Fear* was the go-to manual on recognizing and utilizing intuition, but I couldn't recall any previous works on the care and feeding of intuition.

Within a week, the "article" grew to over thirty thousand words. It wrote itself in torrents. A book about using the deeper parts of the brain was written almost entirely by those deeper parts.

So, welcome. This is a book about living as closely as possible with and from the deeper parts of your mind. I'll explain all that, to the best of my ability, a little later.

To the best of my ability—no book can be perfect. This one won't even be close. I'm trying to write in words about the part of our brains that doesn't think in words. Trying to lay some groundwork in an area with very little advice from the past to build from. So this can never be a definitive work. It's more like a monkey with a vague idea of how to use a branch as a lever trying to pass on the knowledge without a language. Take what's in here, build on it, make it better and pass your insights on.

Introduction

It's easy to say, "Trust your intuition." Words are always easy. But "Trust your intuition" is advice that raises a question. Raises a lot of questions, actually. What is intuition? Why should I trust it? How do I know, or learn, if my intuition is trustworthy? What if there's something wrong with my intuition? How would I know? The list of questions is pretty long. That happens when people give vague, meaningless advice without themselves knowing what they are talking about.

So let's get that out of the way first.

What is intuition?

From the dictionary app that came with my computer:

noun
- *the ability to understand something immediately, without the need for conscious reasoning: we shall allow our intuition to guide us.*
- *a thing that one knows or considers likely from instinctive feeling rather than conscious reasoning: your insights and intuitions as a native speaker are positively sought.*

Intuition, as most people understand it, is just a bubble of information floating up from the subconscious. "Knowing without knowing." Hunches. Feelings with no obvious source.

Did any of that help? It shouldn't have helped. It's all bullshit. The things people babble when they don't really understand.

Caveat— this is my understanding and it may be just as much bullshit as the phrases just listed. This model works for me and I trust it, but that is no guarantee of truth.

Generally, we're looking at this wrong. "This" being the way our minds work. Most people think the conscious mind is who they are, the subconscious a shadowy supporting player. Important, but not as real as consciousness.

That's almost completely backward.

The words in your head, the mind that you are aware of, is less than the tip of the iceberg. The words in your head, in your conscious mind, are just like the words on the computer screen: a tiny effect, almost a side-effect, of everything else going on within the computer. The words are primarily important (whether in your head or on the computer screen) because that is what other humans can interact with.

Your subconscious mind is you. Your conscious mind is largely the story you make up to fill the emptiness in your life.

So when we talk about training the subconscious, we can't really do that. Your subconscious is not only stronger, but smarter than the conscious you. Your subconscious is smarter than I am. It's very hard to train someone who is already smarter than the trainer.

When we talk about training any part of the subconscious, we are really talking about three things. First, getting the conscious mind out of the way. Second, feeding your intuition good information. And finally, cleaning out toxicity. More about those below.

Getting the conscious mind out of the way means letting the real you have a bit more freedom. Yes, the real you. The pure you. Don't read into the words. The real you is not the 'you' you were before your parents messed you up. Not the 'you' that you would have grown into if you hadn't been bullied or had that lucky break. It's the 'you' you have grown into *with* all of the bruises and damage and heartbreak and betrayal you have survived. And also every sunset, and act of kindness, and friendly puppy. It is the 'you' that has learned. Not the 'you' that has interpreted and twisted that learning. It is the amalgam of your experience.

Some people find the idea of a subconscious true self scary. If they let their true nature express, if the little voices in their heads weren't constantly chirping about what other people think and what other people might say, they might become serial killers or violent assholes or... One of my friends, Steven Barnes, points out that every recognized path to enlightenment begins with extensive moral training. Because once you become the pure you, once you remove your attachments— whatever you want to call it— you're pretty formidable. Nigh-unstoppable. The ancients wanted being good to be habitual before you became uncontrollable.

Steve's mostly right. It is powerful. But that other stuff is also bullshit.

If you became your pure self, got rid of the voices in your head, would you be bad? Only if you're bad already. Your conscious mind rationalizes your subconscious decisions far more than it influences them. If you turned the voices off, your internalized morals won't change. You, including your morals, are the product of your experience. Not the product of your rationalizations.

Here's the deal. Most people do the right thing most of the time. Usually for one of four reasons:

1) Hope of reward
2) Fear of punishment
3) It's the right thing to do
4) It's actually easier

If hope for reward keeps you well behaved, you aren't good. You're a mercenary, and probably a cheap one. If fear of punishment keeps you well behaved, you aren't good, you're a coward.

Some people do the right thing simply because it's the right thing, even when it is difficult. This is basically morality as a discipline.

For one or all of these four reasons, most people are good, most of the time. Most of the things that are involved in good are beneficial to your life and to others. High water raises all boats. This is more obvious without the rationalizations and self-talk, not less.

Anyway, I'm not worried about it. In this model, mercenaries are selfish assholes and they rarely have the discipline to develop any real skill. Plus, they're usually too arrogant to listen to someone else. And the cowards mostly put the book down because the voices in their heads are too comforting a norm to ever give up. So I trust that the majority of people reading this are pretty good people. Or at least okay.

I'm going to go deeper, and to some extent contradict myself. Hope of reward and fear of punishment are not the same as reward and punishment. Reward and punishment are real things and affect the intuitive brain. Fear and hope are unreal. They are expectations.

Being good makes sense. Most people are good and follow a moral code (either an internal one or society's) simply because it makes life better and easier. It's not hope of reward; it is reward. Life is easier and smoother when you aren't an asshole.

Conversely, being a dick is usually punished. Having no friends is a punishment. Being a jerk increases friction. It makes everything else in life harder.

There are exceptions. If being an ass has gotten you what you wanted, it has been rewarded, and it is a deep part of your core. But for most of us, we're good people and that makes life better. Friends and allies make for a safer and more rewarding environment than competitors and enemies.

From this brain model, intuition isn't just something bubbling up from beneath the surface of your "real" mind.

Intuition is how you perceive and assess when your conscious mind and your social conditioning and your weird little insecurities aren't fucking with you.

Distinguish between intuition and awareness. Perception is what your senses pick up. Awareness is what you notice. Intuition is about letting your subconscious take the wheel. At low levels, it is about getting your subconscious mind to shift more of what you perceive to your attention, to your conscious mind. But the part of your brain that is intuition is not just for sensing. It also acts more efficiently than your conscious brain, depending on your ability to let go.

When I started writing this book, my intention was to focus on the sensory aspect of the deep brain. But it's impossible to separate just the senses out. Perceiving with the intuitive brain necessitates thinking with the intuitive brain, which will make you move from the intuitive brain. Perception, process and action are not naturally separate things. We learn to separate them. It requires effort to separate them.

> Pro tip: Enlightenment is not something you achieve and find. It's what is left over when you jettison your bullshit.

The second aspect of training is to feed your intuitive brain good information. To see, hear, and smell with minimal cognitive interpretation. This is the other half of the same problem. Your conscious mind can not only suppress or twist information coming from your intuition, but it can twist and pollute the initial input as well. Your deep brain can't always distinguish between what you perceive and the interpretations you attach. The better you get at experiencing without irrelevant interpretation, the closer your cognitive and intuitive brain will align.

The third aspect of training intuition is to clean out toxicity. We are all products of our environment. Many people want to believe that intuition is a magical force that is always pure and always right. It isn't. If you were raised in a toxic family, your intuitive mind learned toxic signals. The baseline established by your experience absolutely colors your intuition. So when you wonder if your intuition is wrong, the answer is, "probably, sometimes."

As a rule, your bad intuition will never go completely away, just like memories. But they can be reinterpreted and replaced with better information.

To be fair, being raised in toxic environments can be a superpower. Living close to the bone can give you a deeper understanding of every other level of need (thinking Maslow's Hierarchy). Living in an environment with high stakes and low margins of error really clarifies both your awareness and your reactions. But those reactions are often inappropriate in a less toxic environment. Unfortunately, reactions ingrained in dangerous situations are difficult to change— the intuitive brain knows that any change could mean death, so it sticks to what has worked in the past. Whether you call it code switching or recalibration, people from toxic environments can and often must learn the skill of adjusting their intuition to the current environment instead of the past.

CHAPTER ONE

The General Problem with Training Intuition

The only reason intuition even exists as a concept is because we spend almost all of our time in our social Monkey brain. We are tribal creatures, social primates, and as such we are obsessed with our place in the community. Alone we die, but in groups our chances are much better, and so even when no one else is present we are trying to make other people happy.

So we look at what society tells us we should look at, even if it is unhealthily cadaverous women with excessive collagen. And we process what we are allowed to look at so that we think about it in tribally approved ways. For example, most supermodels are a weird combination of hairless, emaciated bodies and enormous breasts. How much television and how many magazines did it take to make prepubescent + starving + lactating the modern ideal of beauty?

And we process the influenced observation mentally, wondering which of our thoughts are acceptable and which are not.

Except for the observation itself, almost all of this happens in our minds. It's not real. But it is normal. Almost everyone does it, and if you don't, you will raise eyebrows. The one thing the Monkey brain is really good at is keeping other Monkey brains comfortable.

But if it wasn't for this mechanism, this seemingly magical ability called "intuition" would just simply be how we perceive all the time. Intuition is what your brain and senses are already doing ALL THE TIME. Your social conditioning acts as a filter to suppress your natural way to perceive, and it is so good at it that we are amazed when our brain occasionally functions the way it is meant to.

This is the part where I say, "Stop getting in your own way." End of the book. Easy-peasy.

Nope, that's just as much bullshit as yelling at people to calm down or telling people to use situational awareness without telling them what to be aware of. It is true, it's just not useful for most people.

Overthinking is not natural, but it is normal. And if you've spent your whole life practicing something, just being told that it's wrong is useless.

We have a little edge, though. Within the self-defense community, intuition has a certain cachet. People like having it. So that's something.

Couple of things before we get started:

First, animals learn through play. You're an animal. Go play with this stuff. Life isn't a spectator sport and you'll never get good at it from the sidelines. Play.

Second, I have an assumption. I believe most people are curious. It's fun to keep your mind exploring. So that is one of the positive rewards I'm counting on.

CHAPTER TWO

Before We Begin

It's important to start with definitions and models. That's the only way to be sure we are talking about the same things. Intuition may not mean the same thing to you as it does to me. Do you see a difference between the words "unconscious" and "subconscious"?

Foundationally, we need to talk about *words and symbols.* Our conscious brain works with words and symbols. It really likes words and symbols. You can solve a lot of problems at this level of abstraction. The territory is never the map, but it is pretty damn hard to build a skyscraper without blueprints. Just be aware that there is another, deeper part of your brain that can't always tell the difference between the symbol and the actual thing the symbol represents.

Taxonomies are systems of naming. There is a lot of power in how we name things. If we named all the plants in the world, that would be a mess of random symbols, hard to remember and even harder to really use. But if we organize the plants into their healing properties and name them based on those properties, we'll start to see patterns. The plants themselves will be easier to remember. Connections between plants hidden in the random taxonomy might emerge. Conversely, if we name and categorize the plants based on their genetic relationship to each other (as "binomial nomenclature," or Latin names of plants and animals attempted to do before we even understood genetics) we will see different patterns. If your taxonomy is based on beauty, you will see yet another series of patterns.

Taxonomies are powerful, but they are also limiting. When you are thinking about plants as medicine, you will miss the combinations of beauty.

Operational definitions. Words mean things. Unfortunately we have a nearly infinite universe of things to experience and an extremely limited number of words to describe the universe. And our language isn't all that efficient. We have a lot of synonyms, and if any one word were truly accurate, synonyms would be a waste. The thing is, we can only share the world in words, but we don't experience it that way. Words and symbols are important, but they are just a vague shadow of experience.

I'm going to be using and defining words here, but these are operational definitions. That means that you and I agree on a meaning, for the purpose of this book, so that we can understand each other. If I define something here, and it's not the way you learned the word in school, that's perfectly fine. In school, use your other definition. For here, many of the models are built around operational definitions. Also, trying to communicate in symbols about living without symbols is kind of hard. Meet me halfway.

I use a lot of different and often incompatible models for how the brain works. Incompatible? Yeah. Like taxonomies for healing plants and beautiful plants are incompatible, both are useful in the appropriate context and neither are perfectly true.

Freud's old Id/Superego/Ego model. In this model, the Id is the bestial you— all of your angers and lusts and dark desires. The Superego is your higher self, your conscience and desire to be good. The Ego is your conscious mind, the referee between the two, yadda yadda yadda. This model presents your mind as a battleground between good and evil with poor you in the middle just trying to get by with minimal neuroses. I don't personally feel that my animal self is inherently bad or my social conditioning (where my conscience came from) is inherently good. The assumption that they are opposed doesn't fit my experience either.

Subconscious/Conscious. I do use this one. For my purposes, the conscious mind includes everything you are consciously aware of; the subconscious mind is the rest. I realize that is a circular description, but that seems to be unavoidable when describing a thing to itself. So in this model, the words you are reading are conscious. Any sensation you notice is conscious. The words in your head are conscious. The things you imagine are conscious. All of the things you are actually smelling and hearing but don't notice are subconscious. The time pressure you are in no way aware of that is building up right now about whether to continue reading or do the dishes is subconscious, until the subconscious kicks the conclusion to your conscious mind. The process (of almost all of your thinking, actually) is subconscious. The results of that thinking are conscious.

By the way, reading about subconscious pressures may have brought them to the surface. You may want to put down the book and go do something. That's okay.

Unconscious and subconscious. I catch myself using these interchangeably. When there is a difference, I think of the subconscious as actively controlling you and the unconscious as the background noise. For instance, your unconscious is passively noticing the color of every house you drive or walk by. Your subconscious is gauging how soon you will get hungry and when to start looking for food. All the while your conscious mind is driving and maybe holding a conversation.

Intuitive brain. For our purposes, the intuitive brain is the subconscious brain given control. The goal of this book is to help you shift away from pretending that your conscious controls your subconscious. Sometimes I call the intuitive and/or subconscious brain the "deep brain."

The triune brain model. The science behind the original triune brain theory has been thoroughly debunked, but it is still a very powerful model. Many behaviors become clear if you think of the mind as divided into three levels—the Lizard, the Monkey and the Human.

The Lizard deals with personal survival. It is the part of you that is a perfect animal, not beholden to or caring about others, with no hang-ups or doubts. The emotions it feels are fear and joy. The magic it believes in is ritualistic; if a behavior has not gotten you killed, the Lizard will ritualize and repeat that behavior. The Lizard learns through punishment and reward, through failure and success, with no rationalization interfering. In the modern world, the Lizard is rarely triggered, but when it is, the Lizard has the seniority to completely override the other two brains.

The Monkey is our social and emotional brain. It is the part that is always worried about what others will think. The Monkey is the part that feels almost all emotion. The Lizard feels existential fear of death while the Monkey feels all the other flavors of fear. The Monkey, too, learns through success and failure but measures those through the eyes of the tribe, not through an objective standard. The magic it believes in is symbolic. The Monkey often has trouble telling the difference between narrative and reality, or distinguishing the symbol from the thing. This is the basis for sympathetic magic. To curse your name is to curse you. To damage a doll made in your image is to damage you. To the Monkey brain, this is just the way the universe works.

The Human solves problems. It is the youngest and weakest of the brains and is almost never in charge. That's generally only when the Monkey is satisfied enough to be asleep, or on the rare occasion when survival is on the line but the Lizard has no good solution and there is time to think, such as in a wilderness survival emergency. The Human emotion is curiosity. Not the Monkey curiosity of "What is that shiny thing?" or "Can I eat that?" but the Human curiosity of, "How does that work?" and "What's really going on here?"

Touched on this above, so I should distinguish <u>theories, models and heuristics</u>.

Theories attempt to explain how something works. They are an attempt to get at the underlying truth. If you know the underlying truth of any given event, that event is predictable and manipulable. In humans, if you understand the reason, the behavior is predictable. If the behavior is not predictable, you have mistaken rationalizations for reasons. Theories are tested by testing their predictive power, including whether changing a variable will predictably change the outcome.

Models attempt to get to the same predictive power as a theory without attempting to get to the truth. A model needs to be workable not, in a strict sense, true. My favorite example to distinguish between theories and models is this: Does the sun rise in the east and set in the west?

Of course not. As a theory, that idea is completely wrong. The theory is that the earth spins, which makes the sun appear to move. As a theory, "The sun rises in the east and sets in the west" is completely wrong. But as a model, the phrase is so useful that you can navigate and tell time with it.

A heuristic is a short rule of thumb. It applies to specific incidents and doesn't pay respect to the nuances that theories and models need. "Buy low and sell high" is a heuristic. "People who kill children are bad" is a heuristic.

We talked about punishment and reward above and it will come up again. I use the operant conditioning model for this: Behaviors that are rewarded increase. Behaviors that are punished decrease.

People's definitions of reward and punishment are different. Spanking is a punishment for most, a reward for some. Your own brain probably has different definitions of punishment. Which affects your behavior more: the pain of stepping on a sharp stone or the embarrassment of being laughed at for your reaction? The Monkey brain, especially, can hold humiliation to be a more severe punishment than pain.

Reward and punishment come in two flavors each and the language is very specific in psychology. Positive and negative don't mean opposite. Negative reward is NOT punishment. Positive means presence and negative means absence. If your friends laugh at you, that's positive punishment. If they ignore you, that's negative punishment. If they throw a party in your honor, that's positive reward. If they say, "Don't worry about the check, I took care of it," that's negative reward.

Negative reward is the weakest of the four possibilities. It can be effective when it is concrete. If there is an immediate and obvious painful or frightening stimulus that you remove, the chain of causality is pretty obvious. Pain compliance in handcuffing works on the principle that when the arrestee quits struggling and lets the cuffs go on, the pain will stop. That's cool.

In what passes for nature (modern society), intuition is difficult to develop because in the real world, it is usually reinforced negatively. Some of the exercises that follow work intuition with positive reinforcement. That should make it easier.

The last model (I think) we have to cover for this book: Orders of assessment.

At the base level of the pyramid, at the level of the purely intuitive brain, you get a stimulus and you react to the stimulus without your conscious mind even engaging. You hear an explosion, you hit the ground (if you have certain life

Social

Comparitive

Naming

Intuitive

Orders of Assessment

experiences). You find a rock in your shoe, you pull your foot out. You do this all the time. You're breathing right now.

The second order is simply naming. You get the stimulus, you name the stimulus, you respond to the stimulus. At this level, you find a rock in your shoe, you say, "Ouch" and you pull your foot out. (You're still breathing right now, but you're thinking about it, because I mentioned it.)

The third level of assessment (comparative), people start to bring in their experience and question their senses. You feel a rock in your shoe and you think, "How did a rock get in my shoe? Is it a rock? What if it's a piece of glass? Remember that time…"

A fourth order assessment adds a social level: What will people think if I just pull my shoe off right now? What am I supposed to do? Wouldn't a real tough guy just tough out having a rock in his shoe? (Pro tip: answer is "no.") Why does this stuff always happen to me?

The goal of the book is to help you experience and, as much as possible, live in that first order of assessment. So let's begin.

CHAPTER THREE

The Magic 8

Over the years, the age of 8 has come up in three significant and related ways.

The first time, I was informed that third-grade teachers, the ones who generally work with eight-year-olds in the US, are nearly 100% reliable in picking out which of their students will grow up to be criminals. It was many years and quite a few concussions ago, so I don't even remember if this was something I heard or read, or how reliable the source was. I just filed it away as an interesting possible fact. Poking around while writing this, I found a study by Capra, et al that may have been the source. It's in the bibliography.

Years later, thanks to Malcolm Gladwell's "Revisionist History" podcast, I learned of Eric Eisner's YES program. Many elite universities have full-ride scholarships available for bright kids from shitty backgrounds who live in shitty environments, and those scholarships go begging. Turns out that by the time a smart kid is or should be thinking about colleges, his or her energies have been directed at surviving in the real life shitshow of home and school and maybe dealing drugs and crime.

Smart kids adapt. They learn to survive and sometimes thrive in the gang/crime/drug culture. And once that has become your expectation for normal, it is damn near impossible to unlearn that set of truths—especially if the lessons came at a high price—and relearn another entire way of being.

In the podcast, the sweet spot for YES intervention was third grade. (To be fair, I just checked their website and that says sixth grade.) If you want to give a child alternate ways of being, you want to start early. About eight.

The third corroboration came from survival instructor Toby Cowern while we were tracking an otter in Sweden. "Kids eight and under tend to survive. They get tired, they sleep. They get thirsty, they drink something. They get hungry, they try to eat something but if it tastes bad or burns, they spit it out. Around nine years old, they start worrying if the water is safe. They reject food because it doesn't look like the food they're used to, or they eat things they shouldn't because it looks good even if it tastes bad. Our bodies and brains evolved to survive. Eight-year-olds listen to that. Older than that, they try to think and remember instead of notice."

That matches my Search and Rescue training. Some little kids live because they pretend to be animals. "I'm cold. I'm going to pretend to be a bunny and find a nice warm place to burrow." Whereas some older people actually hide from the searchers, as if they are pretending to be trapped behind enemy lines. This is an interesting rabbit trail—the people who are having a cardiac incident and hide instead of asking for help. The people who knowingly do dangerous things (drugs, unsafe sex, playing chicken in cars) because they are more worried about what people think than what may happen.

The magic age of eight. It's obviously not a hard number, and I'm not sure if it's a hard line or a gradual change. But up to a certain age, we think naturally. We live in our senses. You eat because you are hungry and you spit it out if you don't like it, if your senses indicate it's not good. Above that age we shift to thinking about what we are supposed to do, what we have been told is right. So people are more afraid of dirty water than of thirst.

Dirty water isn't good. You can get a host of diseases or parasites that might kill you in a week or a month. Dirty water might contain industrial pollutants that might increase your chances of contracting cancer by five percent over the next eighty years. But thirst will kill you in days. Your animal mind, your intuition, has a much better handle on the reality of danger than your Monkey brain. Sort of. More below.

This doesn't mean "empty your cup" or reject grown-up knowledge and devolve back to your inner child. This is to use your senses at the primary level.

What does that mean?

You pull a root and bite into it. Immediately your tongue gets a weird, burning but numbing sensation. You spit it out. That's the primary level. The secondary level is thinking, "I don't like this." And that's okay. It's unnecessary, but it is just putting words to the sensation. This secondary level is acceptable because it is personal. The tertiary level is trying to tie the sensation to previous experience. When the experience is relevant, this is fine. "Numbing is really common in nerve agents and a lot of plants have natural pesticides! Spit it out!" When the experience is not relevant, such as "I didn't like whisky the first time I tried it either. This isn't too bad," that can lead to some really bad decisions. The thing is, if you knew which of your experiences were relevant, you wouldn't be putting a random root in your mouth in the first place.

The fourth level is to base your decision on what you think you are supposed to do. "This tastes awful, but I don't want anybody to think I'm chicken, so I'm going to swallow it." The fourth level is the where most people make their decisions. I don't think I'd mind this process if it were conscious, if you went up through the levels and chose the outcome.

Let me walk that out. Most people live at the fourth level and it is habitual. As such, they are largely controlled by an imaginary peer group. "What will people think?" "What will people say?" Even though most people aren't the least bit interested. Even though if they did care, they'd probably be supportive anyway.

The third and fourth levels can be useful if the problem is actually affected by those levels. If you have relevant experience, the third level can help you make a more informed decision. If you will have to explain yourself to a superior, then taking the fourth level into account makes sense. In some situations, reputation management, the consummate fourth-level skill, is the real goal.

The existence of the fourth level makes sense. We live in a world where many things are extremely safe. Far more safe and comfortable than our brains and bodies were evolved to deal with. For most people, most of the time, being perceived as a chicken is a greater threat than being poisoned. Our brains work off of what is punished and what is reinforced. When food supplies are safe and wild animals (and people) rarely maraud, our brains learned that the fourth level is what is punished or rewarded. So much so— and this is the primary point of this chapter— that we are not even aware of the primary level sensation.

This is so common that people who live in their senses appear (need a good word for this— magical? Mystical? Otherworldly?) when, really, they're just being good animals.

I'm about to go down a huge rabbit hole and in the process, I may sound contradictory. Nature of the world is that things are true or not based as much on context as on fact. So here goes.

There are environments where the fourth order interactions absolutely intersect with the Lizard brain. When you are living in an extremely dangerous environment, surrounded by people for whom violence is a normal way of life, reputation management is a basic survival skill.

Most of the people in the US and Europe, the people who generally read what I write, are comfortable, well-educated, safe. For them, the fourth order reactions are wasteful artifacts of an earlier time. But those artifacts would not have evolved without value.

Change the environment slightly and "what other people might think" can become an over-riding tactical consideration.

It's now below. (Remember I said "more below" a few paragraphs ago?)

Your Lizard brain has a better handle on immediate danger, while your Monkey brain has a better handle on social danger. But focusing on danger isn't necessarily useful. If you are obsessed with danger, you live in fear, and that's a shitty way to live.

Living at the primary level also means that you smell your lover. That you really taste and savor your food. That you feel the pressure of your foot on the ground and the texture of your coffee cup. Living at the primary level is immediate, rich, full. Living at the fourth level is abstract, anemic, attenuated. It is barely living at all. In my opinion.

Getting back to a child's mind. It's not about more or less. Adults know more than kids. Hell, you should know more today than you did yesterday. Knowledge increases. It's not about amount, but method. Not masses of information but how you think and perceive.

A kid with eight years of living experience who uses the deep brain (and it's the only brain the kid has) has a survival edge. It's a much greater survival edge to use that same brain with twenty or thirty or forty years of life experience.

Sort of. GIGO. That means Garbage In, Garbage Out. There is a huge mechanism underlying your conscious mind, and that is part of your intuition, too. You are a product of your experience, and there is no way around that. If your experience has been artificial (watching TV, reading fiction), it will color your processing. If your experience has been toxic, it will color your processing.

In Chapters 25-29, I'll give some limited advice on identifying and fixing toxic intuition. For now, I just want to say that third- and fourth-level processing reinforces the bad scripts. Tying sensation back to either imaginary or toxic memory makes the imaginary or toxic seem more real and relevant. "What will people think?" is almost always based on an imaginary community that lives in our heads. If the members of that community are fictional, the results will be incompatible with reality. If the members of that community are toxic, the results will continue the toxicity. It's not a panacea, but a primary step in recovering from either a toxic history or a fictional one is to work as much as possible at the first level of sensation. Divorce current experience from toxic past. See things as they are.

CHAPTER FOUR

Grounding (Meditation I)

I got this from *Psychological First Aid: Field Operations Guide* and it is described in *Training for Sudden Violence*.

Grounding is a system of meditation. I first heard of it as a way to calm children after major disasters. It also helps you get into your senses. And it is very simple:

Shut your eyes.

Name five things you hear. Name five things you feel. Name five things you smell.

That simple. Hearing is the easiest. Right now I hear my wife typing away (and myself, for that matter). The refrigerator motor is humming. A cat doing the half-whine, half-purr that signals he wants attention. My neck crackling as I move my head. A very faint, barely audible high-pitched hum.

Touch is easy too, once you tune in. You do feel your feet either in your shoes or touching the ground, but you aren't always conscious of it. Different clothes feel very different as they settle on your skin. The sense of touch is always there, but generally ignored. Five right now: Cold at my ankles. Forearms resting against the hard wood of the table. Tight muscles in my lower back. Fabric of the seat cushion. Coffee swishing in my mouth.

Smell is the hardest and not in the original exercise. We don't have good vocabularies for smells and that makes them hard to register consciously. Smells are subtle, as well. You'll have to work at it. Currently, I can smell the laundry detergent in my shirt. My coffee. There are two undercurrents of smells— one is wet and heavy (probably from the rain outside), the other light and dry (probably from the dried flower arrangement on the table). And I can smell the warm plastic of my computer.

This is presented as a meditation, and I encourage you to try it that way, but meditations are worthless if they are separated from life. Every so often, no matter what you are doing, stop and listen. Really listen. Your subconscious always is listening, so share that moment with your subconscious. Listen.

Every so often, stop and smell. Just smell. Don't get hung up on trying to name the scents—we don't have a good vocabulary for that. Just distinguish them.

Smell your friends. Don't be obvious about it— it really bothers people when they realize they are being sniffed— but smell people. Smell is possibly the most deeply-wired of the senses. Organisms that haven't even evolved mouths still sense chemicals that are good to absorb. Smell goes deep and gives deep information. Fear sweat, anger sweat, sex sweat and exertion sweat all smell differently. It's possible (likely) that a huge piece of whether two people feel compatible at first meeting is a subconscious assessment of scent.

Smell places as well. There are cities that I don't like because of the smell (and some that have changed; the financial and *embarcadero* districts of San Francisco smell completely different now than they did the first time I visited). There are houses you walk into and feel immediately at home. Probably the scent.

From the blog:

Everything Means Something

When I was working the jails, I would frequently just sit and listen. It was especially important as a rookie. Sit. Turn off your eyes. Listen. Most people talk about "situational awareness" but can't tell people what to be aware of. The next step up (but still weak tea) is to say "establish a baseline of 'normal' and then be alert to any deviation from normal."

Sitting and listening is one exercise to practice finding that baseline. What is the normal hum of conversation? What does it sound like when the shower is running? Which doors squeak? One of the coolest I noticed was spilled kool-aid. The inmates at CHJ would deliberately spill kool-aid just outside the first cell. Once the officer stepped in it on his first rounds, his boots would make sticky sounds for the rest of the night and the inmates could track his movements.

You can and should do this for smells and feelings (drafts, temperature changes) as well. It's a good exercise, both for "situational awareness" and also to ground yourself deeper in your perception. And that's useful.

Unfamiliar wilderness, new city, visiting a friend's home for the first time—I do this a lot. Probably more than I realize.

It's on my mind now because of sailing. I'm not an experienced sailor. Rank beginner, so it's kind of odd that my first serious trip is a transatlantic crossing. Pushes me to be extra efficient at learning.

My first night watch, I was <u>listening</u>. A myriad of unfamiliar sounds. Whooshes and snaps and squeaks and clanking and thrumming and...

Here's the deal. Every single one of those sounds meant something. The squeak, to the captain, meant that the dinghy wasn't perfectly secure. The thump was one wave hitting the hull crosswise from the other waves.

Everything you perceive—everything you see, hear, smell, feel or taste means something. Not everything is relevant and not everything is discernible. But it all means something. And if you are willing to dig in, observe, experiment, correlate, test... you can get skill at reading an area. And also get skill at living closer to your senses. Living deeper in your intuitive brain.

CHAPTER FIVE

Meditation II

I'm not a big fan of meditation the way most people do it. Seated mediation is a beginner tool. It is the training wheels on the bicycle. You should be able to meditate moving, acting, and eventually maintain the meditative state in all of your interactions including (the hardest in my experience) communicating with other people.

The first system of meditation I learned was progressive relaxation. It's easy and effective. Here's how you do it:

- Get comfortable. Probably lying down, unless you can sit or stand without muscle tension. (Pro tip: You can't. Yet. Probably.) Do this in a quiet place. No place is perfectly quiet, so the important thing is no jarring noises, nothing loud, high pitched, or unexpected. Dim lights are best.

- Concentrate on your breathing. In, out. Empty mind is hard, so the beginner thing is to let the words in your head just be "in" and "out" each sound drawn out to match the breath. It should be abdominal breathing, but almost all breathing should be anyway. I've often wondered where people even learn to breathe with the upper chest. How did that even become a thing? Try to fill your lungs completely and empty them completely.

- Tense your muscles in order. Start with your feet. Tense all the muscles in your feet. Maintain that and add the lower legs. Then the upper leg and butt. Then maintain that and tense upwards through your abdomen to your chest and back, out your arms to the fingertips then neck, face and head. Hold the rigidity. If you can, maintain your concentration on breathing while tensing. Hold the tension for a few breaths. How many is a few? Depends. When you first start, maybe only two breaths. It becomes easier with practice.

- Now relax your muscles in the same order. Try to put your conscious awareness at the point of relaxation. As you relax your toes, think about your toes. Try to *be* the muscles, the tendons, the nerves, the bone, the vessels. Let that fill your whole mind. Progressive relaxation is the name. So relax in the same order you tensed— up the feet and legs and abdomen and torso and out the arms and then the neck, face and head.

- Sit in the relaxation for a while. Just breathe. In. Out.

Everything up to this point is partly ritual. Many people need a ritual before they allow themselves to think differently.

- As you breathe in your relaxed state, don't think in words. Instead of thinking the words "in" and "out" just feel the breath coming in and going out. This is easier said than done, but it is the meat of almost any Eastern meditation system. More later.

- You will be distracted. You will hear things you didn't notice before— the ticking of a clock, the hum of an appliance. Acknowledge the distraction and let it go. Don't try to fight it or rationalize it. Those are just more words in your head. Acknowledge and let it go. I used to actually visualize the distraction released into a flow and drifting away.

• Continue for a few minutes.

As I said, this is training wheel stuff. Eastern meditation as a whole gets a big reputation as a major upgrade in thinking. It's actually going back to basics. Most of your brain doesn't think in words. Meditation is trying to silence the constant chatter of third- and fourth-level living. To get your conscious mind to experience (and trust) what your deeper mind is doing 24/7.

If you require a specific environment to use a skill, the skill is probably useless in the real world. Practice progressive meditation via this process for however long you need, but don't get stuck here. If you need a quiet place with no distractions in order to meditate, your meditative practice is pretty much useless.

Practice until you can drop into the profoundly relaxed state without doing the tension first. Then practice the thinking without words first while moving (walking, kata, ballroom dance—pretty much any activity). Then practice until you can drop into relaxation in the midst of a regular, bustling day. Then practice until you can maintain a silent mind in an argument or even a fight.

Do NOT dismiss this. If any part of you is saying it's impossible, that part of you is an idiot. We do this all the time. The trouble is that we make the idea of stillness this unreachable thing that only monks do. All athletes do this. It's called "being in the zone" in high-level athletic training. Or a flow state. You probably do it while driving all the time.

This is not something you build up skills to achieve. This is something you pare down bullshit to return to.

Note—I've been specifying Eastern meditation in this chapter. The West also has a long tradition of meditation, but it is different. The best explanation of the difference I've found is in Allan Armstrong's *Notes on Meditation* (Imagier Publishing, 2011).

CHAPTER SIX

Sitting in X (Meditation III)

This is so simple that it probably doesn't deserve a full chapter.

The exercise is to take a sensation, and simply experience that sensation. Don't try to do anything about the sensation. Don't try to make it go away. Don't try to dig into the feeling. Don't try to understand it.

Next time you are hungry, sit in the hunger. Just feel it. No words in your head. Just be hungry.

When you are afraid. When you are angry. When you stub your toe or your leg cramps. Sit in the emotion or sit in the pain.

You can sit in pleasure, too.

I especially recommend this for people who sometimes get overwhelmed with emotion. Sitting in an emotion without labeling the sensation is immensely powerful, and sometimes healing.

CHAPTER SEVEN

Fasting

I've met people who have never gone a full day without food. When you look at the history and prehistory of our species, that's pretty amazing. Like most animals, we spent most of our evolution hungry.

Of the people I know who have gone a day without food, for most it wasn't desperation— it was recreation. They were either fasting or on a survival course. It's kind of cool, and kind of disturbing, that we currently have the luxury to do for fun what our ancestors avoided at all costs.

Being hungry has three benefits when it comes to training intuition:

1) It's an experience closer to the one we evolved for. The deeper mind you are trying to make friends with knows hunger very well. Hunger wakes it.

2) Hunger is a primary sensation. Sitting in hunger, feeling it without adding the second- third- and fourth-level interpretations, is good practice at living in your senses.

3) Hunger really sharpens your senses. Especially smell. Third day of a fast, you'll be able to smell a restaurant at a considerable distance.

Fasting takes a lot of forms and there are a lot of fads. I'll tell you what I did and do and discuss some other practices, but

I'm not a medical expert. Just because I did something doesn't mean it was smart.

People fast for different reasons. For some it's a social convention. Lent or Ramadan, most people fast because everyone else is and they are supposed to. A few do it for actual religious reasons. In that case it is literally a sacrifice, giving up pleasure to show devotion.

Don't knock it. Every other aspect of love involves sacrifice. Just living with someone involves sacrifice. If you aren't willing to give some things up to maintain harmony, there's no love and you're a selfish asshole. When you postulate an omnipotent being, that being has no needs, so there's no necessity to sacrifice and it becomes a symbolic show of love.

Some fast because they believe there are health benefits.

Some fast because they believe there are spiritual or emotional benefits.

And some fast for the discipline of fasting. I'm one of those.

There are many ways to fast. Or, more accurately, many things that are called fasting. Giving up one thing for forty days. Not eating between sunrise and sunset. Eating every other day.

The fasting I am talking about here is giving up all solid food for at least 24 hours. I do this one frequently, but it almost doesn't count. When I get focused on writing or am off in the desert, it's fairly normal for me to simply forget to eat for twenty-four to thirty-six hours. I also did intermittent fasting for several months (eating on alternate days).

I usually break my fasting down to twenty-four hours, three days or five days. I've only done a five day fast once. And sometimes any liquids (not meal replacements like ensure or protein shakes, but milk was allowed), sometimes clear fluids and usually water only.

As a rule I quit feeling hunger pains roughly twenty-four hours in. Shortly after that, my sense of smell becomes really acute. I notice lethargy about halfway into the third day.

Fasting is something I just did, without any research or much planning. I've been doing it since I was a kid. If you're considering fasting, do some research and think it through. Fasting can be dangerous. Don't fast unless you are healthy enough to fast. Stay hydrated. Don't get so locked into a time limit that if you start to get faint or dizzy you tough it out. Don't pass out while driving. That's just a bad idea.

CHAPTER EIGHT

Figure It Out

Your deeper brain is nuanced. It's not just a simple machine with a simple set of heuristics that gets you from point A to point B faster than your conscious mind. It also gets you there with fewer mistakes. Or at least it does when it has good information to work with.

I've talked about the Monkey brain here, but not the Human or the Lizard. Now's the time.

This is a model, not solid science. Don't get hung up on it.

For our purposes, the Lizard brain is you, the animal. It's your survival instincts. It is alert and awesome, but generally passive. Not by nature; it's just that the problems the Lizard is good at dealing with are pretty rare these days, and like all good predators, the Lizard sleeps when there is nothing to do.

The Monkey is you, the social creature. It's the part of your brain that obsesses about what people would think and about the right things to do. It's in charge most of the time because these are the problems we deal with most of the time. Whether to go to college or not; whether to quit a job you hate and go it alone—most of our big decisions have been made at the Monkey level. You aren't going to starve in today's world whether you leave your job or not. The Lizard doesn't even wake up for that. But your Monkey might tell you it's a survival problem. It isn't. The Monkey is a big liar.

The Human solves problems. It's smart, but it is the new kid on the block. It is slow and weak. The Human brain spends most of its time coming up with logical-sounding rationalizations for decisions the Monkey made quickly and emotionally.

There is a tension between all three of the brains, and the tension often centers on what to trust. The Human brain values reason and logic. It likes things that make sense. You can read a book or take a lesson, and your Human brain will say, "That makes sense, let's give it a try." And that works fine when you're alone. You can try the exact same great idea with an audience and your Monkey brain will step in. The Monkey often decides the new thing is too big a change because it might alter the social dynamics in unknown and maybe unacceptable ways. "Better not to try," the Monkey thinks— and so you either don't execute the idea or you choke. Best example: It is nearly impossible for neurotypicals to logic their way out of stage fright. Monkey brain trumps Human brain.

The Monkey obsesses over maintaining social status— looking cool. The Lizard doesn't give a shit. The toughest-talking blowhard you ever heard might just piss himself when he sees a knife at his belly. The Monkey wants to look cool, but the Lizard knows you run faster with an empty bladder.

All three of these brains are part of the subconscious, the pure self. Don't fall into the trap of thinking that the Human brain only thinks in verbally expressed logic. Just as more than 90% of the time our "verbally expressed logic" is just rationalizations for emotional bullshit, the Human brain solves a lot of problems subconsciously. Famously, August Kekule figured out the structure of the benzene molecule after a dream of a snake eating its own tail.

Your intuition will work best when it is fed by information that satisfies all three of these minds. As a rule, formal learning satisfies the Human brain. To the extent that it solidifies tribal ties, it satisfies the Monkey brain. The Lizard doesn't believe in it at all.

When something makes sense, your Human brain will be okay with it. When something is told to you by an authority figure (however your inner Monkey measures authority) your Monkey brain is okay with it. Your Lizard brain is sleeping most of the time but when it wakes up (usually because it senses danger) it only believes in evolutionary programming or experience.

That's a big problem for self-defense training. The part of the brain that takes over under life-or-death stress doesn't believe in training at all. It believes in freeze-flight-fight because that approach has worked more often than not for many generations.

However, the Lizard is programmed to survive. It can learn, and it isn't stupid.

The simple way around the problem is to survive a situation where the Lizard's default training fails. When the Lizard realizes the inborn patterns will get you killed, it will let you try—in a limited way—your training. If the training works, the Lizard puts those skills in its domain. With a few repetitions of real world success, your fighting comes out without the over-thinking of the Human brain, or the constant worrying and second-guessing of the Monkey brain, but with the animalistic purity and efficiency of the Lizard brain. I really want to say, "Enter the Dragon" right about here, but it's probably too cheesy.

Bottom line: Training and learning is for your Human brain. Sparring and competition is all Monkey. Real survival is all Lizard. Most cases, there's not a lot of crossover. I'll go further: Without integrating training and experience, the Monkey, Lizard and Human frequently interfere with each other.

The goal is to get the three brains to agree. To integrate them. If your consciousness (the weak, shallow, slow part of your brain) trusts the deeper parts (which are doing all of the real work anyway), your conscious will interfere less with your subconscious. You will achieve the "oneness" they used to talk about in cheesy kung fu flicks.

Okay, that was a lot of verbiage to get to this very simple point:

The things you discover for yourself integrate more deeply than anything you are told. Or read. Or whatever.

To the Lizard, experience is pretty much the only real thing.

The Monkey is emotional. We'll save that for a bit later.

As said before, one of the few, maybe the only truly Human brain emotion is curiosity. Not the animal curiosity of "What is that shiny thing?" or "Can I eat this?" The Human brain fascination is with why things work and what things really are. The thrill of discovery.

The Monkey is problematic in this largely because creativity has been so consistently punished. The child who discovers a new color with her finger paints is more likely to be punished for making a

Personally, I pretty much try to negate the Monkey. I'm not neurotypical, and a close friend has described my Monkey brain as an "asthmatic lemur," but hear me out. This gets heavily into my personal ethics and that's one jump away (because it is the foundation) of my politics.

The Monkey has some good qualities. It is why we have friendships and why families stick together and the source of patriotism… There is a lot of good there. But each of those aspects has a dark side as well. The Monkey is tribal, and defines "the good guys" as "my side." Always.

I believe that all things and beliefs that are actually morally good make sense. My Human brain can figure them out. And my Human brain, with reason, can pick out my own hypocrisies. Monkey brain loyalty means standing by your friends even if they are committing atrocities. Human brain loyalty is to choose the team you want to join and to know which lines can't be crossed. Get it? In your Monkey brain, "That's wrong! <Unless my team does it. Then it's at least understandable.>" The Human brain says, "That's wrong. Do it and you're off my team."

Almost everything in society in my opinion can be boiled down to an old psychology game where everyone chooses X or Y. If everyone chooses X, everyone wins a little. If everyone chooses Y, everyone loses twice as much. But if very few people choose Y and the majority choose X, those who chose Y win a lot. X's still come out ahead, but not by as much.

It's a very good metaphor for society. If everyone plays by society's rules, everyone wins. If only a few people cheat (break rules or laws) they profit at the expense of all others. If lawbreaking becomes so prevalent that everyone does it, then everyone loses badly. Side note: If there are too many rules, everyone is breaking some. We all turn into Y's even if we don't want to.

This metaphor applies well, but add this: People don't know the X/Y rules. It is critically important for humanity to have a lot more X's than Y's. So children are conditioned (societal conditioning is what sets the Monkey brain) to be good little X's. That's using Monkey patterns to control.

I see this, though, with my Human brain. I choose to be an X because I can see the consequences if too many people choose Y.

There is a danger whenever society conditions the Monkey without explaining to the Human brain: Monkeys are emotional.

Choosing Y has a lot of advantages. Less effort for more gain. Cheaters do win. When the Monkey sees cheaters win, and not be punished, the Monkey brain notices. When the number of cheaters reach a critical mass, the Monkey brain not only notices, but feels betrayed. At a certain point in any society where there are no or few consequences for cheating (however that society defines cheating) anyone who doesn't cheat is a chump. This is why systems that emphasize equality over liberty and brotherhood collapse.

mess than praised for creating something beautiful. Our deep brains are very much the product of what is punished and reinforced.

Without that damage, a healthy Monkey brain will reject tribal wisdom when confronted by facts, largely because a healthy tribe is endangered by misinformation. But most Monkey brains are not that healthy, and will reject facts to preserve a tribal identity.

Here's the deal.

The closer a group lives to the margins of survival, the less bullshit tolerance that society has. If you see a neighboring group using a food you didn't know was edible or has a medicine that is new to you, you take that information back to the tribe. Rejecting food is a luxury. It takes an immense amount of industrial wealth to survive as a vegan.

The point: Monkey brains exposed to Lizard problems tend to be far more practical and useful. Monkey brains not exposed to Lizard problems tend to think that their emotions and feelings override every aspect of the world, from violence to hunger to physics. This is the Monkey who says, "I feel this subject is so important, I don't care about the facts!"

The exercise for this chapter is to get in the habit of figuring things out for yourself. You already know a lot and you can find out more. I'm not telling you to reject outside learning and sources. I'm telling you to experience things.

Actually do a simple car repair (much easier on an old vehicle). Cook something and change the recipe a little. Look at a building under construction and figure out why things are done in such a specific order. Figure out why bathrooms are usually close together, especially one above the other in multistory buildings.

Walk and run on the beach and look at the difference in your tracks, then repeat the experiment on different surfaces. Experiment and play.

And don't get hung up on failure. Failure is awesome. That's where the good stories and the good learning happens.

Once upon a time…

I was raised in the desert. Where I come from, every school kid does an experiment where you dissolve salt or sugar in a jar of hot water, add some food coloring, dangle a string into the supersaturated solution, and wait for the water to evaporate. When the water is all gone, you have a string of colored crystals.

So, I was thinking about this experiment and got the idea that maybe it didn't have to be coloring. Maybe it could be flavor. So I made a supersaturated salt solution and soaked peppercorns and jalapenos in it overnight.

I wasn't living in the desert anymore and the humidity was high enough that the pepper solution would have grown mold before it evaporated. So I poured the solution onto some cookie sheets and put them in the oven to evaporate.

Failure. Turns out the steam was also intensely saturated with capsaicin. I gassed out my whole house worse than an OC (pepperspray) grenade. I had to mask up to go in and turn off the oven. It took all day to go back in the house. My wife was not happy.

Success. The hot pepper salt tasted amazing.

And now I know the good and bad. Right down to my Lizard.

CHAPTER NINE

Articulation Exercise

This is a cornerstone exercise.

Some background, first.

One of my biggest advantages (though I hated it at the time) was all of the damn reports I had to write. Every time there was a Use of Force I had to sit down and write everything I saw and heard, everything the threat did, everything I did and why. It was a pain in the ass. Especially in the first dozen or twenty force incidents. Memory under adrenaline is unreliable. Things happened fast. Sometimes I had to articulate an event that I remembered mostly as a blur. And I had to write it all down as if I had seen everything and every single motion I made was a conscious decision.

It turns out that I had seen everything and I had made good decisions; they just weren't conscious. When my Lizard brain thought I was going to die, it pushed the Human out of the way and took over. And it did a damn good job. And it never did anything that violated my personal ethics. Your personal ethics are part of you. If your expressed ethics and your actions are out of line, it is your expressed ethics that are inaccurate. Your Lizard will not violate your core values.

Everything was seen, good decisions were made, just not by the part of my brain that writes the reports. So I had to teach myself to replay things in my head. To play back until I could pick out the clues that were so obvious to my deep brain but my conscious brain never registered.

Fights are high-risk, high-intensity, low-time events. And that's nearly a perfect storm to bring your intuitive brain out. Most of you will not have the hundred or more fights it takes before you can play them back in your head. Those of you that do, only some of you will have to write reports and learn this process. But there is a much safer way to get most of the benefits.

The first step is to be aware of your intuition in the first place. Every so often you will "just know" things, or get a hunch. "That driver is going to pull out in front of me." "Something bad is going to happen in this bar." "That kid is going to push the other kid when she's not looking."

The next time you get a hunch and it pans out*, play the event back in your head. Obviously, don't do this while driving. Make sure you're in a place where it is safe to stop, visualize and think.

Play the event back in your head and look for the clues. Your intuitive brain noticed something. Figure out what. Head tilts. Intention motions. Eye contact. Humans are good at reading humans but it is rarely conscious. Work to bring the subconscious to the conscious.

Don't worry if you suck at this at first. To paraphrase Musashi, "You will suck at first, but everybody sucks at everything at first." (The actual quote is, "It is difficult at first, but everything is difficult at first.") Practice. Visualization takes practice. Consciously reading people takes practice. You will get better.

I wrote reports. Writing may help you. It is often more concrete than visualizing. But the real reason it was more valuable may not be available to you: All of my reports were scrutinized. They were double-checked by people comparing them to other reports and, when available, video. Without that,

I think writing and visualizing should be equally valuable, but go with your feeling on the matter. If you prefer to write, write.

*Above, I said to do this exercise on your successful hunches. Part of training is managing fun. You want this experience to be reinforced, not punished. You want to play with your successes for that reason. As your confidence grows, then you can look at your failures, e.g. "I thought he had a weapon on his hip but his shirt rode up and nothing... oh, he's dragging his right leg slightly, tight muscles or lower back pain on that side." Even when your intuition is wrong about the conclusion, it's usually right about the evidence, if that makes sense. But only play with failure after you're pretty confident. For a little more on that see the Chapter 17, People Watching.

The articulation exercise has at least two minor benefits. One is experience at explaining subconscious decisions. It's a minor skill because it is rare, but when it becomes important it can be very important. A lot of self-defense decisions are made very quickly on partial (at least to the conscious mind) information. If you ever need to explain a decision of that magnitude, a little practice is a godsend.

The second minor benefit (and maybe neither of these are minor) is that by forcing yourself to figure out and articulate the clues you get much better at recognizing behavioral clues. Practice at reading people is good, but analyzing your practice of reading people is better. This exercise does that.

But those are minor reasons. Here's the major reason. Intuition triggered is communication from your deeper mind. When your conscious mind analyzes the communication, it becomes clear that it's not magic or telepathy or anything weird. It is solid information processed very quickly. It is *trustworthy*. The more your conscious brain trusts your subconscious, the more you will act without questioning. You become more decisive, especially in high-risk situations.

Once your intuition recognizes the trust, it will start sending you more of these messages. This exercise creates a feedback loop of efficient integration of conscious and subconscious. Practiced diligently, this exercise will literally start breaking down the division between your conscious and subconscious mind.

Practice diligently. From this point on, whenever you get a hunch, articulate it out.

CHAPTER TEN

Let There be Trolls

I'm functionally pagan.

Emotionally, I'm an atheist. The Big Questions™ like, "Why are we here?" and "Is there a god?" don't resonate with me. It's not just that I don't care about the answer; I don't understand the existence or the purpose of the question.

Intellectually, I'm agnostic. Radical agnostic as in, "I don't know and you don't either." The question of religion is ascientific. Postulating a creature who can alter time lines or change causality is the perfect non-disprovable hypothesis. The only scientific response is to not care. Put it another way—if this is all a big simulation *and* we're just very advanced AIs in a game, guess what? All atheists are wrong, there is a supreme being, a creator, and this is all intelligent design. And all the people of faith? In our universe, god is omniscient, omnipresent and all-powerful. But in his world he's probably a dweeby cubicle rat who can't get laid.

Atheism is also illogical, which is a different thing than ascientific. You can't prove a negative.

But functionally, I'm pagan. It's a worldview that satisfies my Lizard, Monkey and Human brains.

People, as a rule, like to have a handle on existence. They like to believe that they understand the universe, and if they understand it, they have a better chance of controlling it. The universe is terrifyingly big, full of forces that can and will crush us all (no one beats time) and more complicated than the Human brain will ever understand. That last is just math: If there are two human brains in the universe, that's twice as much data as a single human brain can handle.

At one point in our history, we used ritual and sacrifice to have good hunting or rain or to prevail in a raid. At another, we believed in a god who would make everything work out in the end. Currently, many believe in governmental systems that will bring a world of perfect peace and justice.

None of it has changed. Not even many of the details. Environmentalism for some people is an apocalyptic religion with its own dogma and prophets and original sin and missionaries and even dietary laws. A nearly perfect corollary to the Christianity many of them reject. The blood sacrifice to the prophet Marx has killed more people in the 20th century than all of the religious wars in all of human history combined. Look it up.

The Lizard brain doesn't care. It does believe in magic. In high risk situations the Lizard remembers every detail of what you did and said and in a similar high-risk situation will repeat some or all of those actions. That's why some people do or say the same things over and over in a deadly force encounter.

The Monkey brain is the big one. The more scared the Monkey is, the more it wants some big Monkey to be in charge. It's the one that believes that a god or a president or technology or nature or a conspiracy is really running everything and we'll all be okay. If the Monkey can't find a god/universal philosophy/whatever, it will manufacture one. And it will lead the true believers to do all of the things that true believers have done in the past.

It is not and never has been about the nature of the belief. The evil has always come from the arrogant self-righteousness of the believers. Earth Liberation Front terrorism is no different than Muslim terrorism is no different than the Spanish Inquisition. The only difference is the authority each had. AntiFa and the Brownshirts are the same group.

The Human brain does, or should, recognize that it is all metaphor. Some metaphors are more powerful than others. (You can measure the power of a metaphor by its predictive power). Some metaphors allow you greater affordances than others. If you believe that your rituals are the only way to get an effect, you don't have the affordances to try anything other than your rituals—and that is exactly the same for monks spinning prayer wheels for peace as it is for bureaucrats following "best practices."

Let there be trolls.

I've yet to meet an indigenous people who didn't believe that there were other intelligences. The spirits where I grew up. Djinn and Efreet in Arabia. Elves in Iceland. Trolls in Scandinavia.

Skepticism appears to be a disease of cities, a product of luxury.

If you spend time in nature alone, you will see and hear things that seem to contradict your ordered reality. Most are explained away quickly. You might be sure you saw a small human moving but as you get close, it was just a stump. Eyes play tricks, everything's fine…

This chapter's exercise is simply to not explain things away. Let there be trolls.

The deeper mind works in different ways. For one thing, it tends to comprehend in lumps or gestalts. Whole ideas or whole stories that pop into your mind. The characters of fairy tales work significantly better in stories than vagaries of air pressure and relative humidity to explain strange sounds.

Humans, for as long as we have been humans, have been story-telling creatures. It is one of our primary learning modalities. We remember stories better than lists. We find connections in anecdotes better than formulas. Our deeper brains work this way.

Humans are also pattern recognition machines. This goes for our conscious and our deep brains. There is some danger of creating a pattern where none exists, but very often our intuitive brains see subtle patterns. It lets us predict the future. Sometimes, when the intuitive brain catches a hint, it will send you a story. And sometimes that story involves trolls. Or Fey, in my case.

Once upon a time...

I'm kind of an idiot in this story. I was climbing Mt. Adams in southern Washington state solo. Wasn't supposed to be solo, but my climbing partners both bailed. I'd been planning this for a while, really looking forward to it, so I thought, "Screw it. I'll climb that sucker by myself."

So I finished my swing shift, grabbed my gear, drove for a few hours, slept for a couple of hours and started the hike well before dawn.

Mt. Adams isn't technical climbing. It's basically a long uphill hike over snow, ice, and boulder fields. It is over 12,280 feet elevation, though. That's 3473 meters.

So I was hiking solo, without acclimatizing (I'd came from 50 feet elevation), while exhausted. I had an ice axe but forgot crampons. Oh, and I'd done my little trick for regular hikes of freezing my water bottles. It never got warm enough for them to thaw, so I was dehydrated, too.

It was a long, bitter, uphill hike in the cold. Fucking miserable. Well below the top, I was sucking wind so hard I had to stop and catch my breath every ten steps or so. The summit was in reach, finally, and I made the last push.

And it wasn't the summit. It was the false summit, a minor peak that hid the top of the real mountain. Made it and saw a snowfield in front of me and 600 more feet of elevation to go. I started across the field and stopped. What the hell was

I doing? I don't even like mountain climbing. It's a miserable fucking hike in the cold and all you get is a view of some shit you were right next to before you started. This is bullshit…

Then I heard whistling and yelling. The voices were faint, but there were three people and a dog up near the summit. They were waving me on. Shouting encouragement. Telling me not to give up. There was a guy wearing a blue down jacket, a blonde woman in a red jacket and a brunette in a green jacket. Bouncing all around them was a black lab.

No way was I going to chicken out this close to the summit. Not with girls watching. I started trudging across the snowfield.

Halfway to where the climb started to get steep, I had to stop for air. Young male pride being what it is, I couldn't be seen to stop to rest, not with girls watching and all, so I got out my binoculars to take a closer look.

There was no one there. There never had been. Complete hallucination.

I can explain it away by calling it a hallucination, but I'm not going to deny this experience. For whatever reason, my deep brain (or maybe the Sidhe, whatever) wanted me to see this. Maybe my intuitive brain knew I'd feel bad for the rest of my life if I quit that close to the summit. Maybe it knew I'd tough it out, get to the top, take a nap and never wake up, so it had to send me something hallucinatory so I would catch the hallucination and honorably climb back down.

Don't know, don't care. Much.

Here's the deal. Science is wrong. Gasp! No! But it is. Everything is wrong. All truth has an edge. Newtonian physics works fine… until things get too big, too small or too fast. Einstein falls apart where things get too small. Math works better with physics than biology (1+1=2 isn't necessarily true with rabbits).

Math is very powerful, but it is still just a model and there are lots of different models that describe the world. The model you use changes your affordances, your possibilities for both perception and action. If you insist that only one way of looking at the world is right, your model is no different than any other benighted religion or superstition.

If you insist that your intuitive brain must communicate in the language of your conscious brain, you have silenced your intuition. You have cut yourself off from the majority of your thinking power.

Let there be trolls. Let there be math and science and stories as well. Accept the information as it comes to you.

CHAPTER ELEVEN

Spend Time in Nature

Eh, sort of. A better way to phrase it is "Spend time away from civilization."

Houses and cities are very different from where we evolved. You'd almost expect intuition to be stunted in cities, but it isn't. Intuitive humans are great at pattern reading, and brake lights far ahead can tell the alert person as much and in the same way as deer going suddenly still in a forest.

Cities are especially good for training the Monkey part of your brain. Side effect, it's also good for damaging the Monkey side of your brain. Cities are artificial in the most basic sense of the word. They are a place where the survival problems have been solved by our ancestors and the most basic needs— water, food, warmth, waste removal—are supplied by other humans. Cities are a place where the Monkey can learn that only Monkey problems are real, that it is completely natural to solve survival problems with money or a petition.

For most people, the Lizard brain is a stranger. It rarely comes out, when it does come out, there's usually enough adrenaline that people remember it as clumsy and stupid. It is anything but.

However, in modern life, there's rarely a need for the Lizard's skills. Doesn't mean the Lizard is useless or obsolete. It is ridiculously powerful. Especially when Monkeys sense its presence. If you want the Lizard aspect of your intuitive brain to come out, meet it halfway. Spend time in an environment closer to where it evolved.

Spend time away from civilization. Mechanical things engage the Human mind. Other people lock you into your Monkey mind. Getting away from all that makes room for your Lizard mind.

I have to talk about Maslow's Hierarchy for a moment.

I've written and lectured about it many times, so no detail here. The idea is that the most basic motivations at the bottom of the pyramid are the essential survival needs: Food, water, shelter, not drowning, not being on fire, not being murdered or eaten by a wild animal.

The next level up are the security needs. Making sure you have food, water, and shelter in the future. That no man or animal will try to kill you in the future.

Next level is being in a group.

The next level is having a good place in the group and being valued by the group.

At the top of the pyramid, people who were secure in all four of the lower levels could be whatever they wanted to be. Self-actualized.

You can look at the first level as the basic Lizard problem: Not dying. The second level is the Human brain solving the Lizard problems into the future. The third level, Belonging, is the essential Monkey problem. The fourth level, Esteem, is the Human solving the Monkey problems. Self-actualization, in this model, is what happens when the Lizard and the Monkey are both satisfied enough to nap and let the Human run the show.

No one goes through the steps of the pyramid from bottom to top. Most are born into a family and are loved from birth. We universally start very near the top of the pyramid.

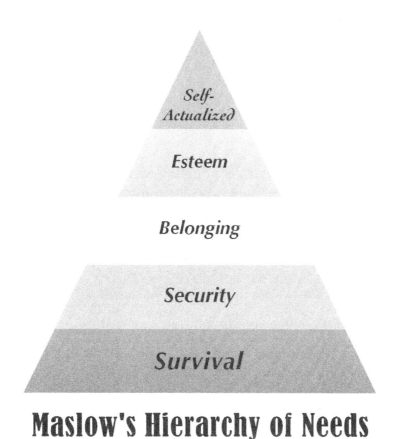

Maslow's Hierarchy of Needs

I believe, however, that without direct experience of the lower levels, our understanding of the level we are on is flawed.

Much of society is designed to make sure that people never have to experience the Lizard issues of the survival level. So we have sanitation and fire codes and grocery stores. If you've never seen a kid with rickets or kwashiorkor, you may know that quality food is important, but without the visceral understanding of why.

Without that depth of understanding, you don't really get why our ancestors were so motivated to put all that effort into the second level. Why we farm the way that we do (and why it is worthwhile to be sure farms have water). Why it is worth digging up the streets to put in sewer pipes.

If you haven't experienced the security level, you can't grasp what a metric fuckton of manual labor it took to feed a family before modern methods. Or what a godsend specialization is when building a house.

When you have worked your ass off as part of a team at something necessary, you understand why belonging is important. You see the power of tribe and team. Without that experience, too often solidarity is just an expression of power for emotional reasons. Not much different than a temper tantrum scaled from a toddler to a mob.

I want you to experiment with a progression:

Go someplace remote, someplace where you can't see or hear or smell humans, and spend some time there.

No communication. No phone or e-mail. Nothing to read (that one is really hard). Not even food labels.

It is hard. A lot of people get this weird mix of frantic boredom. We are not used to silence and want it filled, and want it filled with words and noise...

Stay in that place until you are used to silence again. Look, listen, touch, smell, taste. Use the Grounding exercise. Meditate for stillness if you want or need to, but the key is to get into your senses and out of your head. Try to live in first-level perception.

Meditation retreats attempt to do something similar, but I just find it easier without buildings or human interactions.

Do this. And then do it again. And again. You'll find that each time it gets easier. It takes less time. You'll find a stillness.

This stillness is your intuitive mind. Sit in it for a while. See Chapter 7, Sitting in X.

Next, repeat the exercise, but this time with some challenge or danger. There are generally three things that kill people in nature: Temperature, thirst, or hunger. Almost never hunger, realistically. And falling. Wild animals rarely. (You are way more likely to die by hitting a deer with your car on the way to camping than by a bear, cougar or rattlesnake while camping.)

Don't bring a shelter, for instance. Build one. Or bring no food and eat only what you can find or catch. Use the time in nature to combine Fasting (Chapter 8) and Figure it Out (Chapter 9). Constantly ground to your senses.

This is the part where I have to talk out of both sides of my mouth. The Lizard is smart. It knows simulated danger is not real danger. Want to get in touch with your Lizard? Bring no water into the desert until you're desperate enough to drink out of a hoof print from a seep spring with cowshit all around… but to advise that would not be in keeping with best safety practices. Same with free-solo (no rope) climbing. Danger and deprivation are classic paths to enlightenment, and that's really what we are talking about here.

As much as possible, get a genuine experience of the Survival level on Maslow's pyramid. This is where the Lizard thrives.

The next step in the progression is to do this with other people. Most of them won't do the stillness first, and that's okay. This is about you, not them. They are your lab rats.

In the first stage, ideally, take a survival course together. There are two ways to do this and I recommend you do both. The first is to do this with friends.

Introductory survival courses are pretty easy and safe. Sometimes it's a little cold or they let you get a little hungry, but nothing too severe. Watch how even that tiny bit of discomfort can cause profound changes in personality. After one or two survival courses as a group, take or organize one without shelter or food. Do your due diligence with regard to medical concerns first. Three cold days without food will give your intuitive brain a ton of data on who people are beneath the civilized layers.

In many ways, signing up for a class where the other students are strangers is safer. Friendships sometimes (rarely, don't worry about it) fracture over personality changes. That's not an issue if you take the class with strangers. You can get many of the same observations.

Next (and here we transition from Survival to Security and from Lizard to Monkey), do a team survival class. Teams can build better shelters faster than individuals. Division of labor makes everything easier.

This exercise feeds the Monkey and Lizard aspects of your intuitive brain. You learn about good and bad team work, about people's willingness to sacrifice for others, or scam.

None of this is as intense as the real thing. In a survival course you won't get life and death struggles. Any emergency will be simulated. The work and planning required to survive for a long weekend (which is almost nothing, by the way. Almost everyone can survive for three days just sitting quietly) doesn't approach the labor necessary to prepare a small tribe for a potentially rough winter. But it is a start.

This isn't speculation. I spent my teen years almost completely off the grid. No running water. Batteries were the only source of electricity. We did not have a phone until the second year. It was a party line. My parents had decided that The End Was Near™. Nuclear war, environmental disaster, inevitable economic collapse—the seventies were rife with impending apocalypses.

Being really cold and really sick with medical too far away to reach changes perspective. Self-reliance is no longer a goal, but a condition of life. No one other than the self _is_ inherently reliable. People help because they want to (and that can change), they are forced to (and they will rebel against that), they feel they must (because they feel a tribal bond with you), or you offer something in exchange (and you won't always have or be something they want). None of these are fully in your control, but your self-reliance is.

At the same time, interdependence is not some vague social good—it's a fact. And not always a pretty fact. Solidarity and fascism are the same words. When you are weak or sick or ignorant, you will rely on others for your survival.

No one survives alone for very long. That's a fact. The greater your skills and strength, both the less you need others (and, thus the more choices you have in working with others) and the more valuable you are to those others. Strength, knowledge, understanding, communication, specialized skills—all of the expressions of personal power make you more valuable to the tribe.

Don't get pollyannaish about small tribes and homesteading families. This is about feeding your intuitive brain some knowledge about who people are at the base layers. It definitely isn't all good. Some work and some shirk. Some find betrayal a better source of power than cooperation. Some will stick to the tribal ethics even at great loss. Some abandon those values the moment it is convenient.

Another thing about nature. And meditation.

I never really understood fishing. Growing up, fishing was something we did for food, and I learned to fish efficiently in our creek. I don't like the taste of fish that much, but it was protein.

It was probably watching the flabby, pale 200-pound tourist holding up the 14-inch trout and bellowing, "That sucker put up a fight!" that turned me off of fishing as a recreation.

When I came back from Iraq, one of my friends wanted to take me fishing. I don't like fishing, but I like camping, so we went. We went camping by a remote mountain lake. There were a few other people there. Not many. One was out in the lake, in a floating tube, casting and reeling in and casting and reeling in...

I got it then. Alone. Silent. Floating. Surrounded by nature. Casting. Fishing may be the most sophisticated system of meditation ever invented.

CHAPTER TWELVE

Spend Time Alone

This is subtly different from spending time in nature. I think one of the reasons that it is so difficult to develop fundamental intuition around people is that people are constantly explaining. Every important incident becomes a subject of discussion and soon the discussion is internalized deeper than the event.

We know this from many sources. Memories of events change over time, largely because the way we told our friends about the experience is fresher and simpler than the memory of the event. A few words are far easier to recall than the sights, sounds, smells and feelings of even the simplest event.

Spending time alone is not enough. If you are not used to being alone, it's a challenge. You will want to fill the empty space in your mind. Oh, and know this: If you have things to read and music to listen to and TV to watch, you aren't actually alone. You are still filling your mind with other people's meaning.

Without a lot of practice (one of the things meditation is for, see Chapter 5) you will fill empty space in your brain with your own internal chatter. When there is no one to explain or describe experience to you, you tend to do it yourself.

Being alone is not enough. I want you to spend time being alone in at least three different modes.

Mode 1. Acting. Do not just sit alone and introspect. (There is a time and a place for that. We'll go over it in a bit.) Do something alone. It can be as simple as sweeping a floor. Sink into the sensation. Think in words as little as possible. Just sweep. This exercise crosses over heavily with meditation. (See Chapter 5)

It can be simple, but it is even better if it is strenuous, or technical, or both. Running is an excellent way to be alone, but trail running or rock climbing (just as strenuous but more complicated) are better. Do home repairs. Build something. There is a reason that the home workshop is iconic. A place to be alone and create.

Mode 2. Introspection. I don't think there's usually a good time to just chatter in your own brain. I see little benefit. But that doesn't mean there isn't a time to think deeply. There are multiple states of this, and a practice.

First, I want you to think of a question. It can be deep or shallow, earth-shaking or everyday. "Is there a god?" "Why do I get angry when my wife changes plans?" Anything. Be alone and think about it. Puzzle it out. Use your reason and logic to get to the meanings behind the words. Play with all of the ways you can change the question itself. "Is there a god?" Absolutely, if I define god in a certain way. Absolutely not, if I define it another way. Unknowable, if I define it a third way...

Second stage, bounce between your rational and intuitive mind. Think about the question hard, as above, and then relax. Silence your mind. Passively wait and listen for what bubbles up. Let your intuitive brain play with the question. After an idea or several has bubbled up, go rational on the new perspective. Some of the stuff that bubbles up might appear irrational. It isn't. Your rational mind can weigh the evidence and the pros and cons of the existence of god. Then your intuitive brain might pop in with, "Why is the question important in the first place?"

Mode 3. Every so often shut down your conscious mind and just see what your intuitive mind wants to play with. Let words and images drift across your consciousness. Don't interfere or try to understand, just go along for the ride. I use this when I can't get to sleep. It has the cool side effect of putting me into a dream state before I'm even completely asleep.

CHAPTER THIRTEEN

Work With a Team

Another thing that awakens intuition across the Lizard/Monkey line is working with a team in high-risk situations.

In both cases you are relying on others for your survival. And others are relying on you. Teamwork is in the Monkey domain, survival in the Lizard. Both are parts of your intuitive brain.

If you want to integrate the Human as well, lead the team. Or design the training for the team. Caveat, though. You can have the job title, but unless you go out into the field with the team, you aren't leading it. You're only managing it. You won't get the Lizard aspects. And you won't get reliable Monkey information either. Because people lie.

If you are in a position of authority, people will tell you what you want to hear. You need to be able to see the reality first-hand, or else the information fed to your subconscious is tainted. Same goes for designing courses for elite teams. You have to go into the field with those teams to truly know if your training is effective or if it needs to be modified.

An Aside

Building and protecting are qualitatively different things than destroying. This should be obvious, but it evidently isn't. Working together in survival class or canning food for winter or planning and executing a hostage rescue are all about life. Protecting and preserving life.

If you want to tear down more than you want to build, you're the bad guy. I should probably sugar coat that. Too late.

Here's the deal. The adrenaline and teamwork and intensity is the same for good guys and bad guys. Tactical teams and rioters. Combat patrols and gangbanging. And the intensity is addictive. If that intensity is tied to destruction and intimidation separate from a life-protecting outcome, it is very easy to become a self-righteous violent asshole.

I have to be clear, here, and you have to be clear as well: Working with a team in a high-risk situation means that you share the risk and the work. That is the way for your intuitive brain to access these benefits. Being the cook who feeds the team when they return or the quartermaster who ensures the team has the equipment they need are valuable parts of unit cohesion and mission success, but will not lead to the Human-Monkey-Lizard integration this chapter is about.

In this context, support staff are not part of this team. Nor are administrators or regulators or any of the priesthood of the bureaucracy. And often the bureaucracy is seen as a more subtle enemy. Which can make the group bond even more.

CHAPTER FOURTEEN

The Intuition Experience

This is going to brush up against enlightenment and the experience of enlightenment. Don't freak out about that. There are some weird mystical descriptions and interpretations of enlightenment but it is no big deal. That's a different book, though.

Just remember this—we know enlightenment isn't hard because all animals live there. If a turtle can live in the moment, the problem isn't lack of brain power.

I want to refresh the idea of four levels of living in the world:

1) Living in your senses.
2) Describing or naming your sensations.
3) Tying the sensation to previous experience.
4) Examining the sensation through the filter of your assumption of what other people will think.

Let's do that again:

1) Living in your senses. Stimulus and action with no conscious thought interposed. You feel thirst, you drink.
2) Describing or naming your sensations. Stimulus labeled in conscious thought followed by action. You feel thirst. You think, "I'm thirsty." Then you drink.
3) Tying the sensation to previous experience. Stimulus followed by labeling followed by a cascade of possibly

related thoughts followed sometimes by a decision and only then by action or inaction. You feel thirst. You think, "I'm thirsty. But this isn't as bad as the time I went hiking last summer and forgot my water bottle. That was thirsty. I should probably get some water. Or maybe a beer. I wonder if this house has lead pipes..." Eventually, you might drink and it might be water and it might not.

4) Examining the sensation through the filter of your assumption of what other people will think. Stimulus followed by labeling followed by a cascade of possibly related thoughts then followed by a review of real or imaginary societal rules followed sometimes by a decision and only then by action or inaction. You feel thirst. You think, "I'm thirsty. But this isn't as bad as the time I went hiking last summer and forgot my water bottle. That was thirsty. I should probably get some water. Or maybe a beer. I wonder if this house has lead pipes. Maybe beer then. Is it too early to drink beer? Probably. So I guess I'm stuck with water." Eventually, you might drink and it might be water and it might not.

Being in the moment is the first level. In the Buddhist sense, that is living without attachment. It is pure, fast, and powerful. It almost always gets to the same place as the fourth level, because most of what goes on in your conscious mind is just a shadowy, slow, inefficient echo of what your deeper mind is already doing. That's why I don't worry about doing something I'm ashamed of in a fight. I trust my nature.

There are (caveat— personal experience, there may be much more) two very different ways that the first level expresses.

The one everyone gets excited about is the moment of full sensory engagement when you feel like you are at one with the universe. You don't just hear insects, you hear every insect individually, including some farther away than you should be able to sense. You smell emotion, and the sunlight on water smells different than the sunlight on a leaf and all of the sensations are in you at once. Colors and details, every blade of grass, leaf, hair on a rabbit when you wouldn't have seen the rabbit before...

And the second you say, "Wow," the instant you go into second level, it is gone.

I've only experienced that level on the edge of death, and not every time I've been close to dying. It's rare. Because it is rare and intense, this is what "seekers" are looking for, that satori experience.

It has the intensity of adrenaline-induced tunnel vision (if you suddenly notice a rattlesnake next to your foot, you will see details of the rattler like you've never seen before). That level of intensity, but 360° and all senses. I suspect it is what your mind does when things are both high-risk and ambiguous, when your intuitive brain knows information is the key to survival but can't know what information is the key.

The thing about this level is not that it happens. That's no big deal. The thing is that your conscious mind is allowed to experience where your intuitive mind lives. Right up until your conscious mind starts commenting on it (level 2) and slams the door.

The other level of enlightenment happens all the time and no one notices.

There are things you do every day (probably) at level one. Almost everyone who drives frequently has experienced getting from point A to point B with no memory of the trip. People who drive manual transmission rarely decide to change gears, they just do it.

Want a fascinating one? Reading fiction. When you get sucked into a good book, do you have any sensation of reading at all? Or does your mind create a world as your eyes move across the lines? You don't break down the letters, the words, the grammar and then construct the fantasy world. All of those steps are simply skipped. The sensory perception of seeing little squiggles of symbols leads directly to the action of creating an entire world in your imagination.

Think about that. If our conscious mind were all there was, reading for pleasure would be impossible. It would be a time-consuming, tedious chore.

The goal of meditation (See Chapter 5: Meditation II) is to do all of your tasks at level one. To live at level one.

This practice will counteract the meditation slightly, so don't do it a lot or immediately, but I want you to notice all of the things that you do in level one. All of the times where you are already enlightened. It's more than you think.

Do you touch type? (If so, I'm jealous). Driving. My mom could read and hold a conversation while knitting. It is often easier to spar if you are holding an unrelated conversation. See the next chapter, Rejection and Distraction.

This is the point I want you to experience. When you are working at this level, it doesn't feel like anything. Your feelings about the flow state are second order, and going to the second order knocks you out of the flow state. When you notice you are functioning without conscious thought, the noticing itself becomes a conscious thought and you're out.

So think back, understand the sensation, but don't try to notice in the moment. Like I said, this contradicts the purpose of meditation. Think of it as a gauge, not an exercise.

CHAPTER FIFTEEN

Rejection and Distraction

These are two exercises that I haven't generalized. In other words, I've only used them in limited areas of my life, so you'll have to adapt the basic pattern to areas of your life.

Rejection is a practice for taking a complex skill and making it simple. It is an exercise for skills where you are developing competence but haven't gotten to unconscious competence yet.

In tactical shooting, the elements of marksmanship are stance, grip, sight alignment, sight picture, and trigger press. There are more things, like drawing and moving, but these are the elements of marksmanship. And beyond tactical shooting and going into precision shooting, breath control becomes important. But for pure tactical handgun marksmanship: stance, grip, sight alignment, sight picture, and trigger press.

That's actually quite a lot to think about. You tend to do them in order and usually by the time you are on the final act of pressing the trigger, one of the others has shifted.

Rejection is the practice of ignoring everything you know and just acting.

You have to have the fundamentals down. Stance, grip, sight alignment, sight picture, trigger press. Once you have the fundamentals down, say to yourself, "Okay, let's forget all that" and just shoot.

I've seen this in combat arts ranging from unarmed to small unit tactics. At some point you have to quit remembering what you are supposed to do and trust that the skills are now just a part of you. The keys in that sentence are "remembering" and "supposed." Remembering is third-level thinking. Plus, memory is definitely the wrong part of your brain to try to use in a fight. "Supposed" is a solid indicator of fourth-level thinking. Any time-critical survival skill has to be pushed as close as possible to level one.

So, just shoot.

If you are ready for this level, your shooting will improve. Your groups will tighten up and you will be faster. Better results in less time is a very good thing. You will almost automatically be faster— that just happens when you aren't checking and correcting every little detail. But if you are ready for the rejection exercise, your performance will also improve.

If your performance doesn't improve, it just means the fundamentals aren't fully ingrained yet. Go back to the basics.

Caveat: Would I want a surgeon who practiced rejection? The very idea makes me nervous. But in damn near every high-risk thing I've dealt with, been exposed to, or seen, the truly skilled worked mostly subconsciously, intuitively in the sense we use it in this book. I don't have an answer for how universal this is. I do know it applies to fighting and shooting.

I mentioned unconscious competence, so let's go into that. It's a model for learning skills that has been around for a while.

The basic idea is that there are four levels of skill that you will progress through when learning any new thing.

The first level is unconscious incompetence. You don't know what to do and you don't even know that you don't know. You might not know that the problem exists (your distant ancestors would have no idea about engine repair). You might not think the problem is a problem (really common in failed relationships). You may simply not care.

Conscious incompetence is when you are aware there is a problem, and you are aware you don't know what to do. This is the motivation for learning.

The stage between conscious incompetence and conscious competence is a continuum. This is the process of learning how to solve the problem.

Conscious competence means you know how to solve the problem. But you still have to think about it.

Unconscious competence is the state of solving the problem without thinking about it. This can be high-level skill where an artisan creates in the zone or the experienced fighter who is so skilled he can't teach worth a damn. One of the problems with unconscious competence is that it is really hard to teach others what you do if you aren't consciously aware of it yourself.

There is a fifth level I call the split brain. This is where you let your intuitive brain solve the main problem while your conscious brain is given a task better suited to it. For instance I would frequently let my body take care of the fight (putting an inmate down and handcuffing) while my conscious mind was fully engaged in composing the report.

That may sound mystical, but you do it all the time. It's no different than planning a meeting or holding a conversation while driving.

And that leads into the next exercise, Distraction.

As a rule it is easier to do something than nothing. It is easier to replace a bad habit with a good habit than it is to just quit the bad habit. And it is easier to give the conscious brain something to do than to turn it off.

To make this work, your fundamental skills in the primary task need to be solid. Engage in the primary task but give your conscious mind something else to do.

Again, my examples come from my experience. You'll probably have to modify.

Try this, if you're a martial arts instructor:

Spar with a student. While sparring with that student, watch and coach a different pair of sparring students.

If your fundamentals (sparring in this case) are solid, you will spar better than usual. The coaching puts the conscious attention elsewhere which gets your conscious mind out of the way. You think less, you stink less (in fighting, anyway). It puts the opponent in your peripheral vision, which has a faster reaction time than focused or center vision. Direct vision seems to be wired to the more cognitive part of your brain, so peripheral vision encourages the intuitive brain to step up.

You do better. And, it looks like you are not even paying attention. Does amazing things for your reputation.

CHAPTER SIXTEEN

People Watching

People watching is fun. For those of you who live in cities, people are the best types of animals to watch. Their behavior is amazing and poignant and funny.

The basic exercise for people watching is an advancement of the Articulation Exercise (Chapter 10.) It is called storytelling and is one of the most direct methods of training sensory intuition.

Go to a public place, one with a lot of people, ideally people who are moving. Don't force anything (that's your conscious mind) but let your intuitive mind pick up on someone interesting. It's critical you don't look for interesting. When you actively seek interesting, your conscious mind decides what interesting should look like and then scans for that. It cuts you off from your true intuitive perception.

Let your subconscious mind find someone interesting.

For those of you that are paying attention, this is a method to *create* hunches for the Articulation exercise. Once you have your interesting target ask yourself, "What's the story?" Then let your intuition go.

Humans learn and largely explain the world through story. Your intuitive brain is usually better at reading people than your trained conscious brain. This exercise combines those two facts. Let your intuition tell you a story:

"They're a couple. They've been together for a long time and they go on this walk together almost every morning."

"It's a first date. It's not going well. He thinks he's doing really well and she can't wait to leave."

"That's a fed working under cover." (That one happened in a video analysis.)

Let the story flow. It will probably be simple, not complicated or weird. This is intuition training, not imagination training (though that's good, too).

Then just like the articulation exercise, after the story/hunch, replay the event or observe more consciously and try to find the clues your intuitive brain picked up. This exercise has the same effects as the articulation exercise. Your conscious mind learns that intuition is not magic, and begins to trust intuition more. Your intuitive brain, once it realizes you don't intend to shut it down or dismiss it, will start sharing more. Plus, you will continually learn more

Sidebar on judging. I've written about this in other places but it fits here.

There should be no bad writers. It should be physically impossible to be bad at written communication. Almost every adult in our society has had a minimum of twelve years of professional, targeted instruction in writing. Is there anything else you could have twelve years of training in and still suck? And it's not weekend hobby training. Five days a week, multiple hours a day, for a minimum of twelve years.

Further, writing is not a skill that you practice and rarely use, like fighting. You may not write every day, but you probably read every day. You are surrounded in your daily life by examples of good and bad writing. You practice every time you send an e-mail or leave a note for your kids.

It should be physically impossible to be a bad writer and yet many people, maybe most, are terrible. And here's the deal, they are worse than they would be if they'd had almost no training at all.

Experience. First noticed this when editing *Campfire Tales from Hell*. Some of the roughest, toughest, most bad-assed people you could imagine would approach, shyly, almost apologetically and ask if I might be interested in a story. To which I said, "Hell yes." And they'd send me a story. And it was really good. So I'd call or e-mail and say, "Thanks."

And the bad ass would call me back and say, "No, no, that's not the real story. That was the first draft. Here's the real story." And in every case, *every single case*, the rewritten story was much worse than the first draft.

Here's the deal. The first draft was just a person telling a story. The second draft was a person trying to be a writer.

The trouble with twelve years of professional instruction isn't having twelve years of learning what to do. It's having twelve years of being told you aren't doing it right. Twelve years of judging. And damn near every writer, and all of the poor ones, are more concerned about doing it wrong than they are excited about telling the damn story.

To put it in another context, when the bad asses wrote their first draft, they were just telling a story. That's pretty damn close to a first-level thing. Stimulus: Someone asks for a story; action: you tell the story. The second drafts were all fourth-level stuff. The story was in there, but hampered by every memory of every teacher harping on what elements of a story needed to be there and grammar and…

Imagine a stand-up comedian telling a joke. Now imagine the same stand-up comedian telling the same joke while he's thinking to himself how funny he is. Now imagine the same stand-up comedian telling the same joke while rehearsing the next joke and comparing the laughs he's getting now with the laughs he got in Seattle last month. Now imagine the same stand-up comedian telling the same joke while worrying about who he is going to offend and whether he will get paid.

You can think about consequences in advance, but there is no form of communication that improves when you add orders of complexity in the moment.

All that was to say this: Don't be your own bad teacher. Don't judge yourself out of trying.

about people's tells.

You will have a tendency with all intuition training, but especially with this one, to try to find out if you are right. Avoid that. It is the exactly this second-guessing that suppresses your intuition in the first place. Play the game, enjoy the game.

You can check your story telling skill, if you want, after your confidence level is established. Confidence in this case isn't about accuracy. That would be a circular argument to say that you should only test yourself after you've passed the test. Confidence means that you enjoy the game enough that you will keep playing it even if you are wrong sometimes. When you love the game enough that it's about the game rather than the win, then it's okay to compete.

It would be kind of rude to just drop this here without giving some of the clues your intuition might pick up. I hate it when instructors advise "situational awareness" but can't tell students what to be aware of. So here's the entry-level version of some of the things I look for. Do NOT use this list instead of your intuition. For more, there's a longer section in the book, *Principles-Based Instruction for Self-Defense (and Maybe Life)*.

The first thing I look for is physicality. How someone moves tells you a lot about who they are as an animal. It indicates athleticism, health, old injuries and comfort level with their own bodies. It's one of the ways people with histories of violence recognize each other.

Positioning. There are people who are oblivious to the world and especially other people around them. They sometimes stand inappropriately close to others and don't realize it. There are others who gravitate to positions of power in a room. The power point in the room is usually facing the exits, has a view of a maximal area, limited approaches and is, ideally, elevated.

Proxemics. How close someone stands to someone else can indicate their cultural background and/or the level of intimacy they feel with the other individual.

Eyes. People look at things they like, watch the things they worry about from the side of their eyes, and avoid looking at things that will get them in trouble. The child molester is rarely the guy who looks at kids. He's the one who either hides that he is looking at kids or tries not to look at them. Violence professionals tend to be aware of hands, exits and distance. Victims tend to be aware of nothing at all.

Clothes. No one gets dressed accidentally. People dress to either blend in or to stand out. If someone is dressing to stand out, what is the message? If the clothing message is contradicted by words or behavior, that person is playing a conscious power game.

If the clothes are intended to blend, blend in with whom? Some of the best information is when someone tries to blend unskillfully, for instance a woman who dresses up but doesn't know evening makeup from morning makeup. It shows who the person aspires to be and that she is not a long-term member of that demographic.

Signs of adrenaline and agitation. Visible pulses. Color changes. Tightening or whitening around the lips. Rhythmic movement. Fidgeting. Signs that they have enough skill and experience to control their adrenaline.

Another game, based on the idea that most communication is non-verbal anyway. This one can be done in most large cities, particularly tourist destinations, and it is easy if you travel a lot. While watching strangers in couples or small groups, see if you can follow the conversation in a language you don't understand. It looks a lot like eavesdropping, so don't get caught.

It doesn't work as well if the person is trying to talk to you. The dynamic is different. That said, a few times I've had people hold long conversations with me assuming I understood the words because I'd been able to follow along.

Once upon a time... I was at an antiquities museum in Amsterdam, the Allard Pierson Museum. There was a guy working on classifying some artifacts. He saw me watching, invited me in, pointed out some interesting things and gave a little background. From his tone and gestures I was able to work out that the artifacts were local, from a midden, and that one of the artifacts, a dagger, was probably a murder weapon because it would be very unusual to throw away such a valuable and perfectly good tool. It was about ten minutes into the conversation when he was getting really detailed that I had to confess I didn't understand Dutch.

I was on my game that day. In the same museum one of the guides explained to me how a coffer was used to turn oil and saints' relics into holy oil. He never did figure out I didn't understand his words.

Sounds mystical, it wasn't. The things the guides were explaining were concrete objects and they were right there. Had he only been describing the tap on the holy oil casket, I wouldn't have a clue, but because it was there, almost everything he mentioned, he also pointed to. It would have probably been impossible to follow the same conversations in the abstract.

You can do it in your own language if you are far enough away that you can't hear the words. Or have earplugs in.

CHAPTER SEVENTEEN

You Don't Know

This may take a little background. My wife was showing me a thread on Quora. It was a parent asking for advice. Her daughter was at a sleep-over and the other girls cut her hair off "as a prank." Many, many members of Quora contributed advice, everything from toughing it out to calling the police. And they all sounded so sure.

Simple fact is that everyone giving advice was self-soothing. They were responding to the narrative in their heads— usually a bully narrative. And they were all ignorant.

That's not ignorant as an insult, but as a simple truth. Not a single respondent had any clue about a host of relevant facts.

What was the girl's age? What was her status in the group before the event? She might have been a weak and socially awkward girl specifically chosen as a victim and this was a planned event. Or she may have been the queen-bee mean girl in her school and this was victims' revenge. She might come from a demographic where getting the police involved is normal (though I have no direct experience with such a society even existing). Or she may have been a member of a demographic where involving outside authority is a mortal sin, and I do mean mortal, as in punishable by death.

Everyone had an answer. No one had fundamental, much less complete, information. Ignorance didn't slow the advice. And people in the forum were arguing. Spreading anger in defense of their ignorance. Does that make any sense to you? No? Good.

How often do you do the same thing?

You don't know very much. And a lot of what you do know is simply wrong. And that's okay. Be willing to be wrong.

At best, right and wrong are second-order estimations anyway. In practice, they are usually fourth order. We do not believe we are right because we have truly engaged with our senses, seen how different options worked or failed and then judged the outcome. Our "rights" and "wrongs," like our "goods" and "evils," are almost entirely based on our guestimations of what our tribe would approve or disapprove.

Feeling right, insisting on being right, forces us into the consciousness and forces us to discount any information that contradicts our narrative. It actively cuts us off from intuition.

Let yourself be wrong. Carry around no belief that you hold to be true. Your deepest belief should be labeled, "Stuff That Has Worked So Far." Never more than that.

One of the hardest things for rookies to do in report writing is to distinguish observations from conclusions. Second- third- and fourth-order assessments are all conclusions. (I think I just said report writing is good intuition training. Sigh. It is. Double sigh.)

So rookies write, "The suspect was angry." The experienced officer writes, "The subject was breathing heavily. I could see a pale line around his lips and a vein pulsing in his temple. He tensed and raised his right hand with his fist clenched..."

You are going to draw conclusions. We all do. Those conclusions, whether logical or derived from intuition, will be better if the inputs are better. That means closer to first-level. Understand, and this is a crucial concept, your intuitive mind works off input, not magic. Each of your higher-order assessments are also inputs. Your subconscious hears your judgment. It hears you replay experience. It hears you questioning what others will say. This is one of the things that contribute to the intuitive brain's mistakes.

Remember the children's game, Telephone? The 1-4 order assessments are essentially playing telephone with yourself.

CHAPTER EIGHTEEN

Fly! Be Free!

In case you're a little slow, this book isn't really about training intuition. That would be like sending a gorilla to strength training. The majority of this book is about:

1) Increasing the quality of the information your intuitive brain gets.
2) Getting your conscious mind to trust your intuition so that you can act on your impressions and hunches.
3) Training your conscious mind to get out of the way.

One of the most effective ways to get your conscious mind out of the way is to go into situations where you don't have any experience. Think about it. Third and fourth level assessments are predicated on having previous experience you can match. Without previous experience, you are stuck at primary and secondary experience. And for our purposes, that is a very good thing.

Anchoring into the sensory experience of a thing or event is awesome. Understanding it as pure fun (or fear, that's real, too) is also pretty awesome. This is the "child's mind" or "beginner's mind."

There is a force that has worked on us from the moment of our conception. It literally affects every single action we make and always has. It is so entrenched that even when we are training to combat it directly (and all of weight lifting and most of structural engineering is a direct assault against this force) we rarely think about it. Gravity.

If you are sitting while you read this, were you aware of the sensation of gravity pulling you into the chair? If you're listening when you walk, are you aware that every step is a controlled fall and every transition of weight over your foot uses skeletal structure to fight gravity?

Of course not. We don't think about the things we do constantly.

I called the chapter, Fly! Be Free! That's not the exercise. That's the sensation.

It is hard not to think about gravity while flying. I've parachuted, paraglided and been allowed to take the controls on a small aircraft. I haven't hang glided, or soared. What I have experienced is amazing. The sensation of running in air is amazing. You launch a paraglider while running down a slope with a modified parachute trailing you. When your speed gets to the right point, the chute is going forward while the slope continues down and you realize you are still running but your feet are no longer touching the ground. And flying the chute is like… words fail. Soaring like a raptor. Flight, but silent except for the wind.

Your brain can't turn off, at least not at any level of experience I've yet reached. I'm solidly in conscious competence here. But you have to search for thermals to keep elevation, know how fast you are dropping, how fast the wind is moving you and the limits of your maneuverability, and keep track of good landing places. It is a very Human brained activity, so it is not thoughtless. But your Monkey and Lizard brains have no evolved context for this, so your intuitive brain sits in the experience of it, and what I always experienced as the intense joy in that experience.

There is another, easier (and far less expensive) way to experience flight. Hit the water. I'm talking scuba and snorkeling.

People float (in general). And that reverses everything our brains and bodies know about gravity. In daily life, going upwards takes energy and going downward is free. In the water, staying down takes effort.

Scuba and snorkeling are flying the way birds do it. You can soar or drift to an extent, but movement takes effort. You can move almost equally well in all three dimensions.

It also distorts your senses. Being underwater in the dark can be extremely disorienting, and that can induce panic. Your inner ear canals still know which way is up, but your eyes don't and we rely on our eyes way too much.

Hearing is different. There's an impression of silence, but almost no silence at all. Water transmits sound better than air, but it has a different quality. It transmits different sounds, like clicks, very clearly, but most sounds are muffled, and we have trained our brains to think of muffled sounds as less loud. Do the Grounding exercise under water. Except for the smell part. Don't do that under water. It doesn't end well.

There is a joy in the freedom of movement. Often, your Lizard brain will come out under water, because we've all seen movies with sharks. And there is another place it can come out too, which can be deadly.

I find scuba very slightly less effective for this. Scuba requires a fair amount of skill to be safe. It allows your body to do things that can get it killed (the bends) and preventing the bends requires constant attention to either a dive computer or, for the really old school who were trained to use dive tables (that's me) a watch. That's a lot of thinking.

The other thing, where your Lizard brain can kill you: if anything goes wrong, and you panic, your hindbrain will want to breathe. Your hindbrain knows that air is above the water. Your hindbrain has eons of evolution that says when breathing is difficult, you clear your mouth. People who panic underwater have a tendency to spit out their regulators. I lost a friend that way. RIP, Brad.

Scuba is fun, and you can stay down long enough to see and do amazing things. But you do have to think.

Snorkeling (free diving) is much cheaper, requires far less equipment and, when it kills you, it kills you in a much more organic and natural way so you don't have to think as much.

> One of the big obstacles with self-defense training is that the part of your brain triggered under stress doesn't believe in training.
>
> One thing that I believe helps to overcome this is high-risk training in situations that we don't have evolved mechanisms for. Like being 20 meters under water. When you feel that first wave of panic, your hindbrain might say, "I got nothin'" and lets your training work.
>
> When the training saves your life, your hindbrain gets a glimmer of the idea that training might not be a useless, new-fangled thing. It inches towards trusting other training in other areas.

Goal setting is a conscious brain activity, so this isn't quite the right word, but my goal for my intuitive brain when snorkeling is to hit the place where I don't know how long I've been under and I feel no oxygen deprivation.

This is one of those enlightenment things where the instant you become aware you've hit the level, you will lose it, but it is still the goal. You'll know you've been under for quite a long time, for what seems like an impossible amount of time, but you were just in the moment. And don't worry—your intuitive brain is very focused on survival. It won't forget to breathe completely and let you die.

Pro tip: This is a hell of a lot easier to do in warm water. I find cold not just distracting but obsessively distracting.

Combining snorkeling with Spend Time in Nature (Chapter 12.) We used to (wow, this book is really turning into a list of things I used to do. That could bear some thought) do underwater hiking. We called it Bullfrogging. The idea was to find a nice stream and snorkel for a mile or so, drifting with the current. Hiking underwater.

Snorkeling and scuba can be high-risk activities. Get good training. Don't over-estimate yourself. Practice in still, non-poisonous water. Understand why dams and weirs kill so many people, and that undertows don't just happen in the ocean. Learn to read water. Watch out for hypothermia as well. Cold makes you stupid, stupid makes you dead. And dehydration. Dehydration when you are immersed in water is a sneaky bastard.

Panic story. Not sure where it goes, but this is how my conscious brain relates to my intuitive brain under stress.
Once upon a time… I was solo caving. I know it's dumb. Just like the Mt. Adams weirdness, I'd made arrangements with friends (hmmmm, I think they were the exact same friends, too. Bastards.) and when they bailed, I wasn't going to waste the day.
The last cave I wanted to do that day was Pickard's Sink. Pickard's Sink is unique in that it is a circular lava tube. You go in the entrance and you can just keep going and get back to the same entrance. Impossible to get lost. You'd think.
I saw a tube-in-tube. Tube-in-tube caves happen in a lava tube when a secondary lava flow partially fills the tube and the liquid magma flows out, creating a second lava tube inside/under the main lava tube. It looked big enough to crawl, barely, so I ditched my pack (with the food, water, extra batteries and extra lights) and crawled through. The tube didn't dead-end and popped up under a pile of breakdown. Cool. Pickard's Sink is a circular cave, so I decided to just keep walking until I got to my pack and/or the entrance.
So I hiked over a lot more breakdown than I remembered until I hit a wall. A dead end. You can't have a dead end in

a circular cave. The panic started. It felt like a rat scratching at the back of my mind. I turned around and went the other way. Another dead end. The tube-in-tube hadn't paralleled Pickard's Sink but was part of a different cave.

I was trapped with a headlamp and a handlight. No food or water and the way out was buried under one of the many, many piles of breakdown that had fallen from the ceiling over the years.

The rat scratching at my brain started to get very insistent. So I sat down and had a little conversation. (Yes, I talk to myself.)

"You want to panic. I get that. Let's make a deal. Give me ten minutes to come up with a plan. If I don't have a plan by then, let's panic. Run around, scream. Won't do any good and probably break a leg on all this rubble. But shut up for ten minutes and let me think."

To which my hindbrain shut up. And I came up with a plan. Or I probably wouldn't be writing this.

The plan, by the way, was to crawl under every last pile of breakdown from one end of that cavern to the other. If there was no tube-in-tube entrance, I marked the rubble with a three-stone cairn. So if anyone has been in that cavern and seen a bunch of cairns that go from one end and just stop, that was me.

CHAPTER NINETEEN

Negative Space and Significant Negatives

There is a book called, *Drawing on the Right Side of the Brain.* I'm about as artistic as a lump of coal, so the book was way outside my comfort zone. I did the exercises in the book. Still can't draw for shit, but I learned a lot.

One of the exercises in the book was to, first, draw a tree. When you are drawing a tree, you will draw the trunk, the branches and the leaves. Second, draw the same tree, but instead of drawing trunk, branches and leaves, draw the spaces between the leaves. Draw where the branches aren't. The drawing you come up with is recognizably the same tree, but the drawing is very, very different.

Of all of the chapters in this book, working in negatives is one of the few that allows your conscious mind to directly influence and improve your intuitive mind. Our older, intuitive brain doesn't deal with abstractions well. It likes concrete information. It is more programmed to see a hawk than to notice that the squirrels have disappeared.

Consciously working with absence helps your intuitive brain recognize absence.

Absence does come up intuitively. Many times, when you get the feeling something is terribly wrong, the clue was an absence. A sudden silence, a word unsaid, an expression that wasn't on a face. Recognizing what absence means is one of

Living in the Deep Brain

the few things where your cognitive mind has an edge over your intuitive mind, in my opinion.

The original exercise was to draw the space between the leaves, but there are many more ways to play it.

When walking through a crowd, don't look at the people, watch the changing spaces between the people—that's where you need to walk anyway. In driving, the safest drivers are bubble drivers. Practice to maximize the empty spaces around you. If you have space in front, behind and to either side, you can dodge wherever you need. That's cool. But driving closed in on three sides with empty space only on your right is fine provided you know where the empty space is.

InFighting and grappling are largely about managing empty space. Every strike has to move through empty space to be a strike. Standing at kickboxing distance, you don't have to think about it, because it is almost all empty space. At close range, space is the critical element. In grappling, a lot of the escapes involve creating and exploiting momentary empty spaces, and offensive pinning is largely about denying space.

This isn't primarily a self-defense book, but managing voids, or empty spaces, is a critical element that many people don't understand. The default for most people is to fight where the action is, or to overcome resistance.

Fighting where the action is is as simple and stupid as trying to pull a strangling hand or arm away. The hands on your throat are the threat, right? So your first priority should be to get the hands off your throat, right? So you try to pluck the hands off or pull the strangling forearm away.

It doesn't work. Unless you are significantly stronger than the attacker, you don't have the leverage to pull the hands away from someone gripping you. You can't pull a naked strangle (naked strangle is a specific technique, not being attacked by a nude person) off unless you are strong enough to dislocate the shoulder joint with your hands at that awkward angle. The instinct is wrong.

Same with striking sparring. Amateurs try to beat past the hands. The hands (and feet) are the things that can hurt you. That is where you don't want to be. You want to move your strikes through the space where the opponent's hands aren't. That's one of the reasons beating people up from behind is so much easier. That's all negative space. Rick Wilson has recently written a book, *Now You See It, Now You Don't* that goes deep into the use of negative space in fighting.

If you can get behind the threat, that is moving in negative space. If you can escape a taller threat by diving through the gap under his armpit, that is moving through negative space. And every time you pull on an attacking limb to unbalance, you are shifting the threat into negative space.

Significant negatives are the non-physical corollaries to negative space. Those are the things that should be there, but aren't. I have been happily married for almost thirty years, but don't wear a wedding ring. There's a reason for that. If a popular, charming person has no old friends, there is a reason for that. When someone talks about someone close to them but never uses the name, there is a reason for that.

Catching significant negatives is something I definitely haven't wired down to anything close to unconscious competence. Almost every individual negative I notice, is something I have been trained to see. This is something I'll be working on for the rest of my life.

CHAPTER TWENTY

Be an Alien (or Maybe a Baby)

Since we brought up *Drawing on the Right Side of the Brain*, here's another exercise from that book. It's a big game of "Let's Pretend."

Let's pretend that we are aliens. We have been transported to this world from another planet, another galaxy, another dimension. Everything on this world, Earth, is different than our home. We know nothing.

If you didn't know, would you classify a tree as an organism? Using just what is in front of your eyes, what would you actually see? A tree doesn't move, except when the wind blows it. Just like sand. It's relatively hard. There are some rocks that are softer, some harder. It has rings, but so do many agates. It leaks sap, but so does oil shale.

If you did not already know so much, what would you actually see?

How long would it take you to figure out that talking was human communication? And would you doubt it once you see how little communication actually happens? Dogs, cats, and humans— which are the masters? What's your evidence?

In daily life, we actually see very little. We "know" a great deal and that limits our perception. It's not all bad. It saves a lot of time that we already know eggs are edible. Pre-knowledge is useful, but it misses a lot. I'm not encouraging you to live in a baby's brain, to see everything new and question all of your preconceptions for the rest of your life. I'm encouraging you to do it every once in a while. For fun. Primarily because the sense of wonder you regain makes life better.

But it is also practice at working through your levels of assessment yourself, instead of having the fourth level socially conditioned without your permission by people who maybe did not have your best interest at heart.

The habit of seeing things for yourself and as they are doesn't just work when you are concentrating on it. Your intuitive mind does it all the time. The alien exercise merely helps your conscious mind get out of the way. One of the ways to know that your intuitive level sees what is really there is monitoring when your bullshit detector goes off. Someone, and maybe it is someone you respect, tells you a little fact, and sometimes has a study to back it up. Sometimes you will get a feeling, "that's not right." But most people will dismiss the feeling because of the respect, or the fact that there's a study.

Once upon a time, I was taking a class on "Senses" from the psychology department at my university. The textbook told of an experiment where researchers tried to determine where thirst was sensed in the human body.

Their two best guesses were the brain or the liver. So on one set of test subjects, they injected a hypertonic saline solution into the hepatic portal vein, which serves the liver. On another group of test subjects, they injected the solution into the jugular vein, which serves the brain.

So, someone thought up this experiment. The research team thought it was a good idea. The experiment proposal was vetted by the ethics committee and the science committee before the experiment was conducted (I'm assuming, that's the normal procedure.) The experiment was conducted. The results were written up and submitted for publication. The paper went through peer review and was accepted and published. Someone saw the published article and decided to include it in a textbook. The textbook was written, edited, and sold, and wound up as the assigned text in my class.

Nowhere in that process did anyone remember that veins move blood away from the organs, not towards them.

Your intuitive brain will know if someone tells you a "fact" that from your personal experience can't be true. But you have to listen.

CHAPTER TWENTY-ONE

Blindfolded Work

I wanted to call this chapter "Sensory Deprivation Training" but that's not quite right. Cutting yourself off from information is rarely a good idea. Your brain requires good input to make good decisions. That's true for both your cognitive brain and your intuitive brain.

The purpose of blindfolded training is two-fold. (See what I did there?) The first purpose is to remove all of the mental baggage associated with sight from the equation—not to remove sight, but to remove that baggage. The second and probably more important purpose is to increase the value of the other senses rather than to diminish the value of sight.

Those will both take some explanation.

Baggage. Vision is the sense that we use most every day. It gives us incredible detail. It works at ranges from the tip of our nose to the stars. It picks up and interprets a band of electromagnetic waves… it's good stuff. There's a reason it is our primary sense. There's a reason it is the favorite sense of our higher brain functions.

Because it is the higher brain function's favorite, it tends to invoke the higher brain. One of the axioms of fighting is "When you think, you stink." The cognitive brain is simply too slow to be useful in a fight. I've had good success improving fighters by taking their eyes out of the equation. When you look at things, you tend to think about them with the conscious brain, and the conscious brain misses a lot.

Because sight is our primary sense, it is the one we have the most experience fooling. From stage magicians to optical illusions to make-up, we have several overlapping industries based on fooling your sight. Based on using vision to manipulate you.

There are equivalent manipulations in smell (the perfume industry) and hearing (the soundtrack in any movie is designed to trigger specific emotions), but those industries are far less sophisticated and far less widespread than visual manipulation. Other than pickpockets and a few grapplers and infighters, no one I know of practices deceiving your sense of touch.

There are many types of deception aimed at sight. One of the markers of health is smooth, clear skin. We are wired to find that more attractive than ragged, blotchy skin, so some cosmetics are designed to make the skin look smoother and more even. That's actually changing appearance. But there are other deceptions that only work because of third- and fourth-order assessments.

Joseph Henrich published a paper on "The Weirdest People in the World" which pointed out that we know a lot about psychology undergraduate students and almost nothing about people who are not from WEIRD societies: Western, Educated, Industrialized, Rich and Democratic. One example is a classic optical illusion:

Which line looks longer to you?

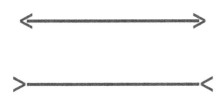

It turns out that this illusion is a product of education. Unless you have been raised looking at illustrations and making three-dimensional models in your head from two-dimensional pictures, this isn't an illusion for you. The lines are obviously the same length. This illusion is a third-level assessment, but one that goes so deep and has become so habitual that it actually presents as a visual distortion.

Another famous psychology experiment, conducted by Asch in the 1950's, attempted to measure social conformity. If you were asked a question with an obvious right answer, but everyone else agreed on a wrong answer, would you take a stand? Or cave?

A lot of people cave. According to the original experiment, roughly 5% of people caved every time. 25% never caved over 18 trials. A third caved at least once over the eighteen trials. This is fourth-level assessment. You have perception, description and history all saying what the right answer is and only the feelings of a tribe pushing you to the wrong answer.

A fourth order assessment can change your perception. That's a problem. And don't get cocky. If you're thinking "Only 5% of the people were pure sheep" or "I would have been one of the 25% who never caved" you're probably full of shit. Remember that this was a tribe made of strangers thrown together for an experiment—not friends, family, colleagues, instructors, officials—And this was an experiment with a very clear right answer:

Which of these lines is the same length as this one?

When the answer is more ambiguous and the majority you need to take a stand against includes people you respect, your vaunted freethinking will probably evaporate.

The second issue. Blindfolded practice is not to discourage sight but to encourage the other senses. When we try to make things equal, it is always easier to tear down the top than to build up the bottom. And it is always a mistake. You have to get things done, every day. That doesn't change when you remove sight from the equation. Figuring out how to do things without your eyes is good adaptability training.

But, as always, there's more. Your sense of smell is an amazing chemical detection system. It works at a distance. Like eyes it is directional, but unlike eyes

> The cognitive brain processes things in words. Which means if you don't have words for something, it is very hard to think about, to communicate about, or to consciously train. This is why most people's earliest conscious memory is from after they started talking. Earlier memories are there, but they don't have the word tags to be recalled to the conscious mind. Most people remember the stories they tell about intense experiences better than the experiences themselves. And good story telling can easily alter memory.
>
> If you have a vocabulary for something, the way wine and whiskey enthusiasts have a vocabulary for flavors, you perceive more intensely and more accurately.

the directionality is based on wind, so it can work on things behind you. It may be as nuanced as sight— it is certainly an older sense— but we just don't spend enough time with it or have the vocabulary to really explore it.

Hearing, taste, touch, smell—all of your senses have a depth of information. Blindfolded training helps you access the possibilities. Your intuitive mind is doing this already. This is another trust exercise to get your cognitive brain to understand the depth and breadth of your intuitive brain.

My primary method of this training is Blindfolded InFighting. There is an extensive section on it in *Training for Sudden Violence,* so this will just be a recap. If you've already read that book, don't skip this whole chapter. I have added some advice for non-combative blindfold training.

Blindfolded InFighting works at one of three speeds. The One-Step is the slowest and safest. In the One-Step, the first partner makes one full-force, well targeted, but slow motion attack. The slow motion is the only safety flaw in the drill. In any live combative drill, you must do something "wrong" so that practitioners can practice without serious injury. That thing you do wrong, like pulling punches? That's the safety flaw. After the first partner initiates the attack, the second partner responds with a single motion of equal or lesser speed. That response becomes the stimulus for the first partner's next motion, and so on. It is a continuous motion drill, but slow and taking turns.

The next level up is flow. Basically, it is very similar to the One-Step except you quit taking turns. It is imperative you don't rely on speed. Work at an agreed speed and stay with it. If you speed up to "win" all you have learned is that you can beat up slow people. If you can hold your own or even win while going slower than your partner, that is efficiency. Above all, the One-Step is an efficiency drill. The goal is to maintain that efficiency as you go into flow.

You can do the flow at any speed, but only at low speeds can you use full force on good targets. I can hit you full force in the throat as long as I am going slow enough. As we speed up, I need to modify power. Unfortunately for real self-defense, the faster you go the harder you ingrain the habit of protecting your partner. People who train fast and hard inevitably become subconsciously better at not hurting people.

The third level is InFighting randori, or free play. It can be done at a range of speed, but the primary difference is in mindset. In One-Step or flow, the goal is not to win, but to solve the moving meat geometry problem your partner is giving you. Your solution becomes your partner's geometry problem, and so on.

InFighting randori is going in to win. As with any sparring, you and your partner need a mutual understanding of what is acceptable speed and contact. InFighting randori is its own thing and can be quite dangerous. I don't recommend you play at high level unless you have experience and confidence, and your distancing and breakfall skills are superb. A lot of the takedowns at InFighting range can really mess up the knee unless you are good enough to relax and take the fall.

InFighting randori itself is good intuition training, especially for physical conflict. Because of the range it is simply too fast and too complex to even attempt to process cognitively. In order to be successful you have no choice except to turn over the reins to the intuitive brain. That also makes it the best way I know outside of real force incidents to get the Lizard brain to trust your training.

Blindfolds can be used at any of these levels or in grappling. You can just shut your eyes, but almost everyone cheats when you do that. For at least the first session of sightless work at InFighting range, I recommend blindfolds. The exercise (described in Chapter 16, Rejection and Distraction) of sparring while coaching is another way to work on part of this skill, but it won't get certain of the benefits.

Blindfolded InFighting works best through a progression. And it's not magic. It's an infighting/clinch/grappling range skill. Blind swordsmen and kickboxers are meat.

Safety first. Clear out obstacles. (I have done blindfolded stuff in environmental work, such as on stairs and with improvised weapons allowed, but only with extremely good people whom I trusted.) As with all training, no live weapons in the training area. Don't blindfold both partners, especially if more than one pair is going at a time. That's just dumb. Control speed. DO NOT go faster than you can control, and DO NOT go faster than your partner can handle. All of your regular training safety rules are in effect. If you do not have regular safety rules, you shouldn't be training anyway. Period.

In the progression, we work defense first. Partner up two people, one blindfolded and one not. Have them clinch up.

The key to gathering information is points of contact. In what I consider a standard clinch (different sports have different clinches for different reasons) my left hand is on my partner's right arm at the elbow and my right hand is behind his neck. (You can reverse right or left here, handedness doesn't matter at all.) That's good contact. I can increase information simply by spreading my fingers as wide as I can on both hands. I can increase it more by dropping the elbow of the hand holding my partner's neck so my entire forearm is resting on his chest. I can even touch my head to his.

You probably don't need to go that far but if you are having trouble, increase the points of contact. This is a life thing, anyway. Whenever you fail, it's a good idea to gather more information. Pro tip right there.

The unblindfolded partner (feeder) initiates a slow, powerful attack, and the blindfolded partner just blocks. That simple. It is important that the feeder not try to be sneaky. If someone is really trying to hurt you, they have definite body mechanics. The feeder's job is to mimic those. A good partner gives a realistic stimulus. Most of the time people are successful immediately. The action/reaction dynamic bypasses the cognitive brain. Most people feel the motion and flinch to a good blocking position.

There are two types of failure to watch for. The least common is the person who comes up with a single universal answer that works for almost everything, like a single big sweeping block that covers most of the body or pushing away the partner at the first hint of motion. These are generally self-correcting. The sweep won't work at speed and pushing away loses contact so you can't see the next one coming and you will get clocked. That said, watch for these reactions, especially the pushing away. It's often the sign of a "fear biter," someone who will panic and flail under stress. Not a good candidate for One-Step, flow or randori while blindfolded.

The second common failure is the person who thinks too much. Sometimes you'll see them start the right defensive action and then abort it halfway, second-guessing themselves. They may also miss or not defend at all. This failure comes almost entirely from fourth-order thinking. The player is so worried about getting in trouble for doing something wrong that they do nothing at all. Usually, this is fixed merely by speeding up. Sometimes, depending on the rules of your class and consent, you can make the unblocked strikes punish. Hurt a little. Pain definitely incentivizes the intuitive brain.

As you get better there are two things to experiment with. You probably don't want to experiment with both at the same time. The first is speed. You will find that as the attacker speeds up, defense gets easier. You think less. If you are doing the striking, gauge your speed. Your job, as a training partner, is to maximize your partner's learning. Go as fast as your partner can handle, but don't overwhelm him. You don't learn much when you're drowning.

The second thing to experiment with is decreasing the points of contact. Doing good in the clinch? Take an arm off of your partner. Try putting one hand on the feeder's sternum with the fingers spread wide. When that gets easy, grab the feeder's wrist. When that gets easy, have the feeder grab your wrist while initiating an attack.

Strangely, I hear people talk about how difficult this must be, but only from people who have read the description but never tried the drill. It is far easier than most people imagine.

Now we work offense. There's a thing that I demo in seminars. I pick someone from the audience. It's not random, but the choice is intuitive. Playing it back in my head the intuitive choice is heavily influenced by how well they did in blindfolded defense, enthusiasm, and relaxation. She puts on her blindfold and I walk up behind. At full arm extension I slap my hand down on her shoulder and say, "Slowly, so that you don't break anything, kick my lead knee." Over 80% of the time, with no training or practice, the kick is dead on. Sometimes I ask for volunteers and it's less often successful. Perfect about a third of the time.

Then I leave my hand where it is and shift my body to one side or the other and give the same instruction. Most of the time, the kick is accurate. Despite the hand in the same place, the difference in tension in the fingers is enough for a blindfolded person to know exactly where my knee is.

The drill is simple. Start from the clinch again and the unblindfolded partner names targets: "Foot" "Solar plexus" etc. The blindfolded partner strikes each target (slowly!). Offense is slightly harder than defense. If your partner misses by even an inch, correct her.

Just like the last drill, as your skill increases, you can experiment with increasing speed and lowering points of contact. Increasing speed in this context is letting the target move. Counterintuitively (to your non-intuitive brain) moving targets can be easier to hit at this range than static targets because movement is information.

When you're comfortable with both of these drills, play One-Step or flow (InFighting randori if you and your partner are really skilled and trust each other.) You can also grapple blindfolded without going through the defensive and offensive steps above.

Many of the benefits of blindfolded training are obvious. For our purposes, though, its primary value is in helping to silence your cognitive brain. When your cognitive brain's favorite source of information is removed, it sort of crawls off in a corner to hide. Kind of like online research experts during an electrical blackout. You have to go old school.

There is a less obvious benefit that really showcases how good your intuitive brain is:

Touch is faster than sight. As you develop skill you will find yourself responding not to the incoming attack, but to the precursors. Most people shift their center of gravity slightly to set up or prep a strike or kick. Any motion, really. For example, before you take a step forward you lean slightly to put your center of gravity over the foot you aren't moving. The shift happens before the motion.

Between the reaction speed of touch and the fact that you act on precursor movements, you will find yourself defending actions before they happen, sometimes before the threat has consciously decided to move. You can almost call it combat precognition.

Bottom line? Most people do better at close range blindfolded. A very few do worse. A few stay the same.

Once upon a time... Above we talked about combat precognition because your intuitive brain can read precursor movements. But it can read a lot more and through a lot more inputs.

A few years ago in Germany I was getting a class up to speed on power generation. They were getting it down and, as a consequence, were hitting really hard. So hard that almost all of the people holding the kicking shields were flinching. That's a problem, because every flinch changes the distance slightly, which is enough to give poor feedback to the striker. So I had the bag holders close their eyes.

And damn near every one of them flinched anyway at exactly the right moment. I have no idea what the intuitive brain was picking up.

Blindfolded combatives is fun and spectacular. But there is more you can do that brings in more senses than just touch. Commit to spending 24 hours blindfolded. This is a double-powered exercise. Unrelated to the intuitive brain, it is a powerful problem-solving exercise. Surviving without sight is something that is very hard, but people have done. How do you get to the store without eyes? Tell if your coffee cup is getting full? Identify the denominations of cash in your pocket? Pro-tip, gentlemen, don't try to pee standing up. Unless you like cleaning up messes.

Your cognitive brain will not like this. Tough. Make it smell and listen. Feel temperature changes (on a cloudy day it is sometimes easier to feel where the sun is than to see it, in case you need directions). Feel the wind. Use a cane as an antenna.

CHAPTER TWENTY-TWO

High-Risk/Low-Time Endeavors

This is just a fancy way of saying doing dangerous things really fast. Dangerous things tend to awaken the deeper part of your mind, but dangerous things that will take a while to kill you (like a wilderness survival situation) allow you time to think.

Danger awakens your intuitive mind. When your intuitive mind is fully engaged and you need your cognitive to solve the problems, it really helps build the unified mind we want. The trouble is that with time to think, the cognitive brain tends to suppress the intuition. That's why we get lost hunters who die because *they don't want to break the seal on their emergency survival packet.*

When you are about to die, right now, and you don't have time to think, you won't think. What comes out will be your animal self.

Here's the problem with that. This is all sampling error. If your life is on the line and you don't have time to think and you think anyway, you die. If you die, we never get to hear your insights on the subject. And that's survivorship bias. Everyone who writes about things like surviving a violent attack from personal experience is writing about what worked for them. And the sample size is so small that you can't tell the effective stuff from the lucky flukes.

Every thing I write in this section is going to be influenced Seeking high-risk, low-time experiences is not a good idea.

Any good, experienced self-defense instructor will tell you to avoid all that you can. One of my personal checklists for people with actual experience of violence is they don't seek it out. Wannabes seek violence.

Here's the deal. You frequently get the kid who really wants to sit at the grown-up table. "But you guys only respect people with experience!"

That's absolutely not true. We respect the guys who get up every morning and put in time at a shitty job to feed a family. We respect the women who call men on their bullshit. We respect the people who share their skills. We respect anybody who sacrifices to make life better for other people.

But, we feel closer to each other. That's not disrespect. Take a good hard look at the old fighters you know. Listen to the joints when they stand up. Watch for the muscle trembles from the nerve damage, or the eyes darting around when they try to remember through the TBI fog. Count their teeth. Whatever scars you see on the outside are more than matched on the inside.

That's not meant to sound whiny.

Try an analogy. It's a lot like being the first few couples to have children in a large circle of friends. Parents, especially

Sampling error and survivorship bias. Sampling error first. What percentage of people in the world have blue eyes? It's a simple statistical question. You could take ten random people from your hometown and crunch the numbers. But if your hometown is Nairobi, Kenya or Reykjavik, Iceland then your results will be wrong. That's sampling error. You see this in self-defense. There are a bunch of instructors who scare people by telling them that the legal system is incredibly dangerous and there is a lot of gray area in self-defense law. They aren't being deliberately misleading. Most are attorneys or expert witnesses. They get hired to figure out the gray areas. If you've worked a hundred cases and all were gray areas you start to believe the world is 100% gray area.

Survivorship bias. To put it in the starkest terms, failure has the best lessons but in life-or-death stuff only the successful get to talk. It's a form of sampling error.

Every thing I write in this section is going to be influenced by my sampling error (my life) and my survivorship bias.

new parents, talk with each other more because there's a big part of their life that childless people can't really get.

Anyway, back to the kid that wants the experience. There are things you can learn in violence and maybe only there. There are things that you can only learn in high-risk/low-time situations. Granted. But not everybody learns them. Some don't survive. Some are so scared that they learn nothing.

And experience isn't a thing, anyway. You don't get to say, "I've been in a real fight, now I'm experienced." It's not a thing; it's a scale, and it's a scale with no end. That's why genuinely experienced people rarely feel they've been tested. No matter what you've experienced, there's worse out there. The only way to know your potential is to exceed it, which is death.

High-risk/low-time endeavors are both a good way to encourage your intuitive mind and one of the few valid ways to test the integration of your intuition and your consciousness. The more integrated you are, the better your chances of survival. The more you survive, in general, the better your integration. Don't think of this as a "chicken and egg" problem. It's really a feedback loop.

Last caveat about high-risk/low-time endeavors. They can become addictive. It's not just the adrenaline junkie aspect, though that is a piece. Internal integration feels pretty awesome. Living without the third and fourth order assessments feels clear and clean in a way that's very hard to find in the modern world. Lastly (maybe— there's no way to know what I don't know or don't yet see) doing something useful and necessary that other people can't do is a huge ego stroke.

CHAPTER TWENTY-THREE

Let Yourself Have Your Wins

One of the most damaging aspects of the way we teach, especially children, is the constant judging. (See the sidebar in Chapter 17, People Watching.)

People are so used to being criticized that when no one steps in to fill that role, they criticize themselves. This is literally insane. Insane in the legal, M'Naghten rule sense where one is legally insane if they are incapable of recognizing an act is wrong or they can recognize that an act is wrong but are incapable of controlling that behavior. You know that constant self-criticism is wrong, but you likely do it anyway.

Intuitive brain, as we have defined it, likes living close to your senses. First or second order. Sensation or simple judgment. "I like it" or "salty." In contrast, the Monkey brain is the voice wondering if you're supposed to like it. The intuitive brain registers that a food is salty and whether you like it, but the Monkey needs to know if it is saltier than it is supposed to be according to largely imaginary outside or "objective" standards.

Right and wrong can be very subjective and they probably don't even exist. The intuitive brain deals with whether something worked or failed objectively. Whether things got better or worse, whether things felt good or hurt.

In training, you should beware of any instructor who has to tell you what worked and didn't. Things that work tend to be obvious and things that fail tend to be even more obvious. But we can easily use words to confuse that issue.

Once upon a time… one of my friends wrote a short story. It was hilarious, obscene, satirical. I still remember it almost forty years later. How do you think a high school English teacher would have reacted to the story? Story-telling is about entertainment and/or transmitting information. It's not about the red pencil. Russ' story served his purpose. Being told his grammar was incorrect or the form was wrong or the subject inappropriate would not only have been irrelevant, it would have actively attacked his creativity.

That's Monkey stuff. Here's something that's not-so-secret about your deeper brain. It likes power. It likes being strong and fast and clever and even ruthless. In the natural world, power is safety. Power is access to food. Every deep part of your brain revels in an increase in power or an exhibition of power. Weakness is unnatural. Embracing weakness, or making passivity a virtue, is toxic and probably insane. Your brain likes being tough.

But one of the things you will notice is that a martial arts student who has trained for years might score a solid hit on a partner and immediately apologize. Immediately feel bad. Go off on a flurry of self-recrimination.

That's bullshit, and if you're observing you'll realize that the shame and fear of punishment isn't an immediate reaction. There is a very tiny time delay. What actually happens is that the student hits and there is a microsecond of the intuitive brain going "Yes!" and a double shot of pure pleasure and pride… and then the Monkey brain steps in and ruins everything.

There's some justification for it. Humans are so powerful and so feared by other humans that it is *de rigueur* to punish them for expressions of power. So in a way the Monkey is protecting you from that. Again, bullshit. If you are in an environment where your successes are punished, get out of that environment.

But even more, for our purposes, distinguish your first, fast, intuitive reaction to your wins and anchor to that emotion. Sit in the glory of success.

One of the hardest things to do in a debriefing is to say, "That went about as well as it could have." When you get a solid win, acknowledge it; don't dress it up or try to tear it down. Let your wins be wins.

Conversely, if you fucked up, acknowledge the mistake, learn the lessons that are actually there, and move on.

Winning and losing aren't binary. There's actually an easy to understand scale. At the top end, there's the perfect win: you gained everything you could hope for and lost absolutely nothing. At the bottom end of the win scale, you got what you needed—just barely—and it didn't cost more than you could pay. If you didn't get the bare minimum you needed, that's a loss. If it cost more than you can pay, no matter how much you gained, it's a loss. At the bottom end of the lose scale, you got nothing and you lost everything. Colloquially, that's called 'dying.'

The win margin is still pretty wide. But it's amazing how often people beat themselves up for anything less than the perfect win. You're still breathing? It wasn't a complete loss. Did you learn anything? Then you didn't leave empty-handed.

Let yourself have your wins.

CHAPTER TWENTY-FOUR

Toxic Intuition, Generally

Your intuitive brain is an amalgam of your nature (whatever that really is) and some evolution, maybe. But it is largely based on your history. The lessons the world has taught you. The behaviors and beliefs that were punished and rewarded.

If your history was toxic, your intuitive understanding of the world will be off. Maybe way off.

I have to be careful, here. It is not that your intuitive brain has been damaged. It has been set for an environment, and when you leave that environment, it must be reset. The equipment needed to survive in an open ocean is different than the equipment need to survive in the arctic. Neither set of equipment is inherently wrong, but it can be wrong for that environment.

Same with intuition. If you were raised in a violent, dysfunctional, family you won't have the intuitive skills to handle a loving relationship. Conversely, if you were raised with love and support, you won't have the skills to deal with a violent or co-dependent relationship.

There are at least two basic intuition problems, and they can be hard to distinguish because the end result looks similar. The end result? Life not going as well as it should.

Don't get me wrong. Life will never be perfect. No one will ever achieve a perfect life. You'd have to make all right decisions, luck into the right opportunities, stumble into the right connections, put in maximum effort all the time and at exactly the right thing... Never gonna happen. That's okay.

But if you're constantly wondering why you make the same type of bad decision, or why you never see a class of problems coming? If you look around at people who had fewer advantages than you but are more successful, then the problem may lie in either your intuitive mind or your response to your intuitive mind.

If your intuition is not calibrated for the environment you are in but you trust it, bad stuff can happen, or opportunities can slip away.

If your intuition is calibrated for your environment, but you don't trust it, bad stuff can happen and opportunities can slip away.

Determining the problem is largely a matter of self-awareness. The last time you got hurt was it because you didn't trust your gut? Or because you did? The time before that? Pretty simple.

Know how you measure success. Giving this some thought can really clarify your life. Some people measure success by assets or income, and that's fine. Money is objective and measurable. Some by popularity. Some by service to others. Some by accomplishments: projects completed, felony convictions, books published...

The particular criteria is less important than knowing the criteria. It's really hard to be happy if you've never figured out what makes you happy.

For the record, I measure my own success by having the best friends and the best stories.

CHAPTER TWENTY-FIVE

Toxic Intuition 1: Garbage in, Garbage out

Contributed by Chiron Training Director Malcolm Rivers

"Garbage in, garbage out," is easy to say but in an increasingly connected, distracted world, this is hard to avoid, practically. Here are a couple of ideas for how to self-regulate and keep your intuitive self from being overwhelmed with potentially toxic nonsense. The first regulatory concept is controlling intake.

If you assume you don't need to manage messaging or that you don't underestimate the power of media, do a simple self-check. Watch a horror movie. Did you jump, cringe, or in any other way react to the completely fictitious depictions of actors pretending to die in unrealistically gruesome ways? Yes? Then you're capable of being manipulated, even when you do it on purpose... to yourself. You momentarily forgot that you're watching a blinking screen, safe in your home, with nothing even remotely dangerous occurring (hopefully) at this exact moment. You got caught up in something you <u>knew</u> was fake. It's ok, it happens to lots of us.

Most media are bullshit: fiction, or fictive depictions of actual events. Much of it serves agendas, not all of which are in your best interest. But unless you're truly committed, you're not going to stop watching movies or listening to music purely on this basis. The key is to control your intake and the first step in that process is identifying what you're being sold.

All stories have messages. The creator is trying to sell you a set of themes, ideas, and/or perspectives. If you thoughtlessly take in these messages, they're more likely to influence your intuitive self. If you can actively practice identifying the themes and messages, you can pretty easily identify what you're being sold and decide whether you want to let it in. You're probably already good at this. Parents do it. A lot. We just get to a point as adults where we assume we can let anything and everything in without any influence on us.

The first time I realized this was when I was a teenager. Back in those days, I could only carry one CD in a Diskman, so I listened to albums over and over again. I'd been listening to a particularly dark album for a couple of weeks and began to perceive its influence on my moods. The world looked like a shittier place when I had some angry, bitter young man rhyming in my ear for weeks at a time. Go figure.

Next time you watch a movie, identify what values the storytellers are trying to promote. An easy way to identify this is looking at how the main character succeeds and fails. If the main character's tragic flaw is cowardice, the story is promoting bravery. There are levels to this and, as you get better at it, compare your impressions with your friends' impressions or, even better, the impressions of honorable enemies. See what you're picking up and how you see it portrayed. You may even notice certain political agendas promoted… but I digress.

(Rory's note: "Honorable enemies" are those rare and special friends who are willing to call you on your bullshit.)

The first exercise naturally leads to the next concept: countering the (potential) garbage intake. It's pretty simple: next time you think you're being fed garbage (or, even better, when you completely agree with the ideas promoted) pick it apart. Find the holes in all of the themes. Turn your emotions off, and your brain on, during the part with the sad music to see what's being emotionally engineered. Actively seek out the places where something is unrealistic or ideologically inconsistent. Identify what's off and why; see if you can tie it into a larger message and consider how it reflects on that message. This helps to offset the potential influence of garbage and is also a good way to sharpen your perceptual and communicative skillset. See if you can convince someone doing the same thing from a different perspective. It's also, you know, fun.

The final concept is balance. For every piece of nonsense you encounter, expose yourself to some reality. For every fiction film, watch a documentary, or take a walk outside in the real world. Look up the physics in the fantasy movie, research the footnotes of the documentary. Allow yourself to see the holes and to enjoy the challenges, even to ideas you support. Examine how these messages you're being sold might influence your epistemology or even your affordances and decide whether it's healthy and useful. If not, treat it like junk food and limit your exposure or just cut it out altogether. Your mind is just as susceptible to garbage as your body is.

The summary, really, is keep your brain turned on when you're taking in information, even from seemingly innocuous sources. Someone is selling you something. Make sure it's something you want to buy and, more importantly, that it lines up with reality. Use this process to expand your knowledge and understanding so that your intuitive mind is fed, and challenged, in ways that serve your mission.

Malcolm Rivers

CHAPTER TWENTY-SIX

Toxic Intuition 2: Not Being Played

There are industries that deliberately and directly influence the intuitive brain. Entertainment, advertising, politics... All exist to resonate with your intuitive brain and evoke an emotion or a decision.

These industries have gotten pretty good at it. Especially the news. We all have and will hear stories that get us at an emotional level. I don't care what the emotion is: outrage, pity, anxiety. It goes to our deep brain, our intuitive brain, and it feels real.

Personally, when I get emotionally engaged by an artificial event (anything I see on TV, read on the internet or in a book, or hear on the radio), I stop. I stop and think. I search for the mechanism used. What engaged my emotion? Was it word choice (when is an 18-year old a man vs. a child? Why is this person called a lobbyist but another person doing the same thing is called an agent?). Innuendo. Jumping to conclusions. Even background music can have an effect...

When I recognize the mechanism, cool. That's good practice for my intuitive and conscious brain working together.

If I can't recognize the manipulation mechanism, I assume that the manipulators are better than I am and any reaction I have is untrustworthy. You don't hear about the things where I get irrational not because of my great and wonderful rationality (joke) but because most of the time it's fairly easy to sense my irrationality and I simply don't share that stuff.

One friend thinks this is aberrant. She said that emotional reactions are products of your intuition and are more reliable than your reason. But that's insane. The purpose of advertising is to bypass reason and get the sale. Political parties have known, at least since Westen's research, that rationality is an obstacle to overcome and no political campaign is served by appealing to reason. If people are being manipulated, and they are, it's irrational to trust the product of that manipulation.

I'll go out on a limb and say that a large part of the mess the world is in right now is because of this assumption that feelings are closer to the truth. That's a dangerous assumption when they are so often (and obviously) manipulated.

But the second part is, possibly, weirder. She seemed to think it odd, almost pathological that if I couldn't find the mechanism, I'd assume I was unreliable. She insisted the natural and correct way was to assume that if you couldn't find the mechanism, there wasn't one.

Con artists rely on this. And the scariest and most thorough way to lose, is to be convinced that it's a win.

This goes deep.

CHAPTER TWENTY-SEVEN

Toxic Intuition 3: Righteousness

One of the things that can feel most like intuition are feelings of righteousness. Whether a righteous belief in a cause or righteous indignation over an affront. This is enforced by a society where almost all hero stories are about doing the right thing no matter the odds, no matter what other people say.

Because our feelings of right and wrong are so strong, we rarely question them. We assume that the right and wrong we believe in are, in some way, universal.

That's not true. If there is a universal moral rule it is that life is precious and any healthy human will sacrifice his or her life or happiness for that of their children. Everything else you believe about right and wrong, good or evil, was taught to you. And it was taught to you to further the interest of the society that taught it.

I'm going to push some buttons here, but bear with me on this example.

Social ideas of right and wrong are heavily influenced by resources. Many things that are bad at one level of supply are good at other levels. When there isn't enough food to go around, nature selects for those genes that take care of their own. When people are starving, racism is common sense. Any group that treated strangers as well as they treated their own would lose to those who didn't. The altruists would die out.

But when people aren't starving, the benefits of diversity are immense. A wider, deeper gene pool makes more possibilities. Different backgrounds and thought processes expand discovery, and that is beneficial to everyone.

At a certain level of abundance, racism shifts from a necessity to a stupidity.

It's never quite this clean. We are the products of our history, as well. Sometimes historical "goods" still cling.

For thousands of generations, manhood was based on one's ability to protect and to hunt. And that image of masculinity still lingers and resonates. It was a necessity and we, as humans, make our necessities into virtues.

As thing became more peaceful, the ability to protect became less important, and the ability to provide became the primary attribute of masculinity. To the working classes the manly man did long hours at the factory, was reliable, could do hard and dangerous work hour after hour, day after day. To the upper classes, the same virtue was represented by wealth.

Today, neither of these things are strictly necessary for the survival of the rest of the tribe—the women and children. It is difficult to define a 'good' man or a 'bad' man if you can't anchor it to some kind of necessity.

Do you follow? Because this goes for all feelings of righteousness, our Monkey brain doesn't distinguish between strong feelings and truths, and the Monkey informs our intuitive brain. If you have that feeling of righteousness, either in a cause that you are certain is noble or indignation at a condition you are certain is horrible—if you can't tie that back to a logical necessity, well, it's just an opinion. And one that probably arose to appease your peer group.

There is no truth there. Watch for your flashes of anger. Watch for your flashes of quick approval. A healthy intuition knows what <u>isn't</u> important.

CHAPTER TWENTY-EIGHT

Toxic Intuition 4: The Trend Towards Homeostasis

This isn't necessarily toxic. If you are happy with your life, then avoiding change makes sense. I include it because it is so often a habit and so rarely a choice.

Every organism has a normal baseline. If things get too hot or too cold, fish die. So do people and worms and everything else. Too wet or too dry. Too much oxygen or too little. Homeostasis is the balancing point and all creatures strive to maintain homeostasis.

For humans it goes further. Our relationships tend toward homeostasis. So does our success and our levels of drama and…

We see someone jump from bad relationship to bad relationship and we think, "How odd is it that someone can keep making the same mistake?" But it isn't a mistake. Their intuitive mind is seeking homeostasis, is seeking the kind of relationships they are used to.

Few people are significantly more successful or less successful than their parents. A few are, those who recalibrated their comfort level. But most are not.

I know a man who by rights should be one of the most successful people in his field. He has innovated a number of new paradigms. He has mentored many of the people who are successful. But every time he gets close to the success or recognition he has earned, he shoots himself in the foot. Fails a critical deadline. Undermines a critical relationship. You see, he was raised in poverty and that's where he feels he belongs.

Get this. It's not penance or guilt issues or anything like that. To his intuitive brain, he belongs in poverty the way an alligator belongs in a swamp. It is his nature.

You also have a baseline that your intuitive brain doesn't want to leave. As I said at the opening of this chapter, if your life is happy and your intuitive brain is keeping you in that happy place, I can't call it toxic.

But if not…

I like to think that just pointing out it's a subconscious mechanism will be enough to give people the option to change. But we know damn well that's not the case.

Our intuitive baseline can change. Realistically, many of the exercises in this book are precisely about affecting that change. Slowly and carefully. Especially changing your attitude towards comfort. Making exploring and being a little uncomfortable your new homeostasis.

CHAPTER TWENTY-NINE

Minor Thoughts and Observations

The intuitive brain is the biggest part of who you are. It is the majority of your mind. I'd be a fool to think that a book this size could do any more than scratch the surface. This chapter will include some tinier scratches. Ideas and practices that are too simple to spend a chapter on by themselves.

Let simple be simple. Almost every intense test I've ever had, part of the instructions included some variation of, "Answer the question as it is written. Don't read into it." A lot of things are simpler than we expect them to be. Thirst is thirst. Let simple be simple.

You don't need the third- and fourth-order assessments. Or really even the second, but I'll leave that here for now.

Don't read into the question, and don't read into the answers, either. Those are two separate things. "Am I thirsty?" is a complete question. "No" is a complete answer. Even writing this I want to add qualifiers and dig deeper into the questions.

I'm going to give a real life example. There is one group, we'll call them X, that doesn't want to kill children, not even enemy children. They are a military group and whenever they deem a certain type of military operation is necessary, they risk the success of that mission by warning their enemy to remove the children from the targeted areas.

There is another group opposed to X. We'll call them Y. They find pictures of their own dead children so valuable for propaganda purposes that when X warns of an impending attack, Y announces that anyone who removes their children from the target zones will be summarily executed along with their children.

X is trying to save children. Y is willing to kill their own children for propaganda purposes. This is a simple thing. Y's are the bad guys.

Some of my friends when they look at this want to educate me. "No, the situation is far more complicated than that. There's thousands of years of history…" Bullshit. There is no historical fact, event, or pattern that can outweigh the willingness to kill one's own children for propaganda points.

I'm not saying don't gather more information. I'm saying don't read into the situation. Gathering intelligence is qualitatively different than inserting opinion or guesses into your equation. That's at the question end.

On the answer end. Don't try to put lipstick on a pig. Or gild a lily. Most of you know, I teach self-defense. Most of the things that work in fast, dangerous situations are extremely simple and efficient. I find consistently that when a technique feels "too easy" the students want to add something. An extra grip or strike or twist. It never makes the technique better.

Be left-handed. Or right-handed. Whichever you aren't right now. Do as many of your skills as possible left-handed for a while. Write some notes, open doors, work keys, switch your knife and fork hands.

Switch dominance. I got this idea from an as yet unpublished book by Kathy Jackson.

If you are in the gun community, you know that people aren't just left or right handed, they are also left or right eyed.

Sometimes right handed people are left eyed and vise versa. According to Kathy, there are right-eyed people, left-eyed people, ambiocular people (that's a real word). And some who are "switch dominant."

I'm switch dominant, so I have always assumed it was a choice or a skill. So I want you to do an experiment. Because maybe it's just me.

Part one, determine your eye dominance. Hold a thumb up out at arm's length. Keep both your eyes open. Do not look at the thumb, but focus on something far away. The far wall, or edge of the parking lot, or a tree on the horizon. You should now see two thumbs. If you blink one eye at a time, you'll only see one thumb at a time. Blink alternative eyes and watch it switch back and forth. It's kind of fun. it also tells you which image belongs to which eye.

Part two, open both eyes and focus on the horizon. You should now see two thumbs again. If one of those thumbs looks more real or solid than the other, that thumb belongs to your dominant eye. If they both look equal, you're ambiocular.

Part three, whichever looks weaker, concentrate on it and will it to be the solid one. See if you can switch dominance. Let me know how it goes. I honestly don't know if this is a skill or genetic.

Go barefoot. Here we go. Of all the exercises in this book, this is the one I don't do. It makes sense. The feet are full of sensory nerves. Our feet are our primary connection with the ground, with the earth... but I don't do it.

Maybe because I was raised in rattlesnake country. Maybe because the place I currently live is infested with thorny blackberries. Probably because I'm a big chicken. (Shit, now I have to do it!)

Anyway, Vic Verdier of MovNat recommends it, and he is a smart guy. And it does make sense, as I said. Vic says not to worry about the pain or toughening the feet. Your feet are plenty tough, they just need to be exposed to enough sensation that they quit interpreting everything as pain.

So as an exercise, going barefoot can both increase your sensory connection with the world and also fine tune it away from misinterpreting things as pain.

Wrasslin'. Not grappling. Grapplers think too much. Especially beginning grapplers. Wrasslin', rough-housing, and horse play are natural and probably necessary. The human body is evolved to move, not to sit. Running and climbing and jumping. And the best movement is random. Trail running or bushwacking requires more of you than running on a track.

Further we are, physically and mentally, what Nicholas Tassim Taleb calls "Anti-Fragile." We toughen up under pressure. We improve with hard use. Mind and body. There are limits, of course, things can be shattered. But avoiding hard use dooms you to entropy.

> Okay, right here. There is something supremely dysfunctional in a society that seems to get every possible permutation of the word "love" confused with sex. Roughhousing with children will not turn you into a pedophile or mess up the child later in life. Do you realize how insane that notion is?

Natural movers. Anti-fragile. And the other piece: We are tactile creatures. A baby who isn't held, touched and loved will be messed up. Healthy children from non-dysfunctional families love "wrasslin' with dad."

This may be too late for you, but it might not be too late for your kids. Play with them. Move with them. Let them feel your affection.

Your kids are moving machines. Let them move. Encourage them. Engage their intuitive and play brains with your own to as much depth as you can.

One other thing about wrasslin' and movement. Movement out of context is always sterile. Lifting weights can be engineered, but bucking hay bales works you in a different way. Pull ups will never do the same things as climbing a tree. Dancing alone will never compare to dancing with a partner. Wrasslin' (including the grown-up version, grappling) is the epitome of moving in context while making a connection (sometimes an antagonistic connection, but a connection) with another person.

And this isn't just for kids.

Smell. Smell goes to the deepest part of the brain. It seems (at least for me) to trigger an animalistic and predatory process when I consciously smell a threat. And I'm sure being sniffed in a brawl is a little freaky from the other end. I've found it to be a quick in-the-fight gateway to my intuitive or animal mind. Also, if you can smell, you are breathing.

Consult the Great Potato. I don't remember where I got this from or why it is called consulting the great potato. I know I was very young and it was right after we moved to the country and my parents were obsessively reading books about homesteading.

One of those books advised that if you really couldn't make a decision, flip a coin.

If you want to flip the coin a second time, you know what you really wanted.

AFTERWORD

The Mom Vibe

Frequently, I run 2-day seminars. We start each day with a safety briefing that covers the basics: take care of yourself, take care of your partner. On the second day, we stop and repeat the safety briefing, but I often add, "It's day two," I say, "You're tired. Tired is stupid and stupid is dangerous, so I'm going over the safety rules again. I'm also invoking a special rule: the Mom Vibe."

Moms are great at knowing that something is wrong. They are also great at knowing when something is about to go wrong. If you've been a mom, you know the feeling. If you've had a mom, you've been on the receiving end: "You kids knock it off or someone's going to get hurt!"

I remind the assembled students of this common experience. The Mom Vibe rule is this: If anyone gets a feeling that someone is about to get hurt, don't ignore it, don't dismiss it, don't analyze or question it. Call for a break.

The students nod, but the truth is, if I leave it right there, they will ignore or dismiss the vibe. I'm a manipulative bastard, so I add: "Don't you dare have the effrontery to tell your students to trust their intuition and then turn around and dismiss your own! If you get the Mom Vibe, invoke the rule!"

Don't you dare. Don't you dare to tell people to trust their intuition and then not give them the how. Don't you dare tell people their intuition is reliable without giving them the skills to feed, purify, and listen to their inner voices. Don't you dare insist that your students trust their guts and ignore your own.

Don't you dare.

Works Cited

Armstrong, Allan. *Notes on Meditation* (2012) Imagier Publishing

Asch, S.E. "Opinions and social pressure". (1955) *Scientific American.* 193(5): 31–35.

Barnes, Steven: https://stevenbarneslife.wordpress.com/

Capra, Barbaranelli, Pastorelli, Bandura and Zimbardo. "Prosocial Foundations of Children's Academic Achievement" *Psychological Science* 2000 Jul 11(4):302-6

Cowern, Toby. http://treadlightlysurvival.com/home.html

DeBecker, Gavin. *The Gift of Fear and Other Survival Signals that Protect Us From Violence* (1999) Dell

Edwards, Betty. *Drawing on the Right Side of the Brain* (1989) Tarcher

For information on touch deprivation in infants, start here: Harmon, Katherine. "How Important Is Physical Contact with Your Infant?" *Scientific American,* May 6, 2010 https://www.scientificamerican.com/article/infant-touch/

Henrich, Joseph, et al." The Weirdest People in the World" *Behavioral and Brain Science* (2010)

Jackson, Kathy. http://www.corneredcat.com/

Malcolm Gladwell's Revisionist History: http://revisionisthistory.com/
Specific episode: http://revisionisthistory.com/episodes/04-carlos-doesnt-remember

Miller, Rory. (editor) *Campfire Tales from Hell* (2013) Marc MacYoung

Miller, Rory. Everything Means Something https://www.patreon.com/posts/everything-means-32201109

Miller, Rory. *Principles Based Instruction* (2017) Wyrd Goat Publishing

Miller, Rory. *Training for Sudden Violence: 72 Practical Drills* (2016) YMAA

Musashi, Miyamoto. *Book of Five Rings* Various translations and editions

National Child Traumatic Stress Network and National Center for PTSD: *Psychological First Aid: Field Operations Guide* (2005)

Quora: https://www.quora.com/

Sagan, Carl. *The Dragons of Eden: Speculations on the Evolution of Human Intelligence* (1977) Ballantine Books

Taleb, Nassim Nicholas. *Anti-Fragile: Things That Gain From Disorder* (2012) Random House

Vic Verdier: https://www.movnat.com/vic-verdier/

Westen, Drew. *The Political Brain: The Role of Emotion in Deciding the Fate of the Nation* (1959) Public Affairs

Whitebread, David. *The Importance of Play* (2012) TIE

Wilson, Rick. *Now You See It, Now You Don't* (2019) Wilson Practical Defense

Young Eisner Scholars (YES) program: http://www.yesscholars.org/

Not cited, but:
Crawford, Matthew B. *Shop Class as Soulcraft: An Inquiry into the Value of Work* (2009) Penguin Group

Acknowledgements

We have a saying that professionals don't do dangerous things alone. Not if there's any choice. Writing and publishing a book may not be dangerous, but you still don't do it alone.

My lovely bride is a constant encouragement. She also does the interior design and covers. Pro tip: Your true love is not the one that will make you feel complete or still your soul. Your true love is the one that you will spend the rest of your life striving to be worthy of.

The first readers, Dr. William Kennedy and the Chiron directors, Malcolm Rivers, Dr. Tammy Yard-McCracken and Paul Dirienzo gave me invaluable feedback.

There were also a number of people pushing me to get the damn editing done. Can't remember all of the names and won't try, but thanks to all of you. I needed the push.

Editing. Kathy Jackson is world-class as both an editor and a friend. If you find a typo, you'll know that's a part I added after she looked it over. I totally want to misspell her name right here, though.

Dunbar Lewis asked to be included in the acknowledgements. Here's the deal. I did the final editing while sailing from Cape Town, South Africa to Grenada with a stop on St. Helena. I'm a rookie sailor. Dunbar (the captain) and Irene Voskamp (the boat's owner) made it possible for me to take and survive the trip. We haven't made it to Grenada yet, and there's still a lot of Atlantic to cross, but thank you both (and Edwin) for an epic adventure.

This book is dedicated to my dad, the late Ron Miller. Among other things, he taught me to be still in the woods. I think everything since then has flowed from the ability to simply be still.

About the Author

Rory Miller spent a long time studying martial arts, a career working the jails in and around Portland OR, and a little time as a contractor in Iraq. He's written several books, initially as therapy, later out of habit, including: *Meditations on Violence, Facing Violence, Conflict Communications, Principles-Based Instruction* and *Training for Sudden Violence.* Also some videos. And some more books.

He's privileged to have some pretty cool friends.